A SEAT BEHIND THE COACHMAN

Diarmaid O Muirithe

A SEAT BEHIND THE COACHMAN

Travellers in Ireland 1800-1900

Gill and Macmillan

First published in Ireland in 1972

Gill and Macmillan Ltd
2 Belvedere Place Dublin 1
and in London through association with the
Macmillan
Group of Publishing Companies

© Diarmaid O Muirithe 1972

Jacket design: Desmond McCarthy

7171 0585 7

Printing history
5 4 3 2 1

Printed and bound in the Republic of Ireland by
Cahill & Co Limited, Dublin

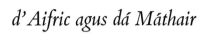

d'Aifric agus dá Máthair

Non laudandus est, quoi credit plus qui audit, quam qui videt;
Non placet, cum illi plus laudant, qui audiunt, quam qui vident;
Pluris est oculatus testis unus, quam auriti decem.
Qui audiunt, audita dicunt; qui vident plane sciunt.   *Plautus*

Acknowledgements

I should like to thank the proprietors of *Punch* and the *Illustrated London News*, the Mansell Collection and the National Portrait Gallery in London and Rex Roberts Studios in Dublin for their help in tracing some of the illustrations in this book, and for granting permission to reproduce them. I should also like to thank Miss F. Clandillon for granting permission to reproduce the translation of the Waterford Famine Song, and Mrs Eilis Ellis and the Irish Manuscripts Commission for their permission to use Margaret McCarthy's letter from New York. I must make special mention of the staffs of the RTE Reference Library, the Linen Hall Library, Belfast, the National Library of Ireland and Trinity College Library, and I am grateful to Dr L. M. Cullen of Trinity College, Dublin, to Professor Séamus Ó Néill of Carysfort Training College, Dublin, and to Mr Henry Heaney of Cardiff University for advice and encouragement. To Mr Pádraic O'Neill and Mr Michael Littleton of Radio Telefís Éireann I owe a particular debt.

Diarmaid O Muirithe

Contents

Foreword

DURING the greater part of the eighteenth century the Irish Catholics, the vast majority of the people, lived under a penal code described thus by Edmund Burke:

> IT HAD A vicious perfection—it was a complete system—full of coherence and consistency; well-digested and well-disposed in all its parts. It was a machine of wise and elaborate contrivance and as well-fitted for the oppression, impoverishment, and degradation of a people, and the debasement in them of human nature itself, as ever proceeded from the perverted ingenuity of man.

In the words of a young lawyer who was to play a major role in the shaping of Ireland in the following century, this code proscribed the religion of the majority, prevented them from accumulating property and punished industry as a crime; it enforced ignorance by statute law and punished the acquisition of knowledge as a felony. By the time it was relaxed somewhat in the final quarter of the century the bulk of the population had been reduced to a state of the most abject poverty and degradation. 'They had ceased to be a nation', wrote Paul Dubois, 'and became instead an inert mass of exhausted and hopeless humanity.'

True, the last twenty-five years of the century saw a great economic progress, in which, perhaps, the lower classes did not fully share; but there was the hope that in time the disabilities under which the poor suffered would disappear through the growing liberality of the Irish parliament, influenced by men of the stature of Grattan and Foster. 'The question is now', Grattan had said, 'whether we shall be a Protestant settlement or an Irish nation, for as long as we exclude Catholics from natural liberty and the common rights of man we are not a people.' Unfortunately, the Protestant ruling class determined to cling to their ascendancy, with the result that the Catholics, despairing of parliament, and adopting the principles of the Revolution, as did large numbers of Presbyterians in the north, rose in rebellion in 1798, shouting slogans from Tom Paine's *Rights of Man* as they attempted to set up an Irish Republic.

But the undisciplined peasantry proved no match for the government's soldiery; routed, they quietly watched the parliament in Dublin consenting to a legislative union with Britain—a union that many of them believed would bring them emancipation at last.

What was actually in store for them was chronicled by many travellers. This book is an anthology of their comments on the Irish scene between 1800 and 1900.

BOOK ONE

From the Union to the Famine

GRANDEUR AND SQUALOR

Almost all the travellers who visited Dublin in the early years of the nineteenth century were impressed by the city's grandeur. Although the Act of Union had reduced its status, it remained the seat of a viceroy, a centre of administrative and commercial importance. A provincial capital, Grattan might call it, but it was still one of the greatest cities in the Empire.

Architecturally it was a handsome place, as handsome as any city in Europe, some said. The wide streets commissioners had done their work well since 1757. Broad thoroughfares, many of them over one hundred feet wide, linked magnificent squares. Brick-mellowed houses of Georgian dignity lined the streets and in the suburbs even the new nineteenth-century terraces displayed an elegance in keeping with a great tradition. The eighteenth-century mansions of the Irish peers and the two main administrative buildings, the Four Courts and the Custom House, strengthened the tourist's impression of Dublin as a city of character; but they were also made aware of the city's continuous growth by some splendid post-Union buildings, the College of Surgeons, the Post Office, the King's Inns and the Castle Chapel among them.

The limits of greater Dublin in pre-famine times were marked on the north and south sides of the Liffey by two late eighteenth-century canals; while the vast expanse of the Phoenix Park prevented any major development to the west. Clontarf, Drumcondra and Glasnevin were then outlying villages; Ballsbridge was a cluster of houses built around two small factories. Within the five square miles of greater Dublin almost 200,000 people lived when Miss Anne Plumptre visited the city in 1814.

Miss Plumptre, daughter of the President of Queen's College, Cambridge,

Above
The Four Courts, Dublin

Right
The Custom House, Dublin

a kindly woman with a roly-poly figure, had previously written some interesting accounts of her travels on the continent. She found Dublin as gay and as bustling as any place she had visited in Europe, but she noticed with regret the conversion of the mansions of the departed peers into commercial buildings and the rapid decay of the fine town houses. In Miss Plumptre's opinion, the city had become a trifle vulgar with the change. She noticed the deterioration of some of Dublin's finest squares and she was appalled by the filth of the Liffey. Said she in her *Narrative*:

WHOEVER SEES the river Liffey, such as it is running through Dublin, must smile at the recollection of Tickel's poem, beginning

> *Of Leinster fam'd for maidens fair,*
> *Bright Lucy was the grace;*
> *Nor e'er did Liffey's limpid stream*
> *Reflect a fairer face;*

since nothing can be more black, dirty, and in every way the reverse of *limpid,* than is the complexion of these waters as they traverse the metropolis. Instead of being an ornament to the town, as a river ought to be, it is really rather a revolting sight. From what cause this may proceed I know not; but it should seem that it must be from very great mismanagement of some kind. Are no pains ever bestowed in cleaning it? or do the sewers of the town run into, and thus contaminate it? I know not whether either of these causes may have any share in the evil, but I know that the magistrates of the town would do well to exert their influence in having the cause thoroughly investigated, and proper remedies applied. It is generally expected that a tide river should be sweet and pure; that the constant ebb and flow should keep it free from impurities; at any rate it should seem as if the cause might with ease be ascertained, and the effect remedied. . .

The area of Stephen's Green is larger than any square in London: it is really a *square,* and is considered as a quarter of an English mile every way. On my first arrival in Dublin, the centre was a green enclosed round with a live hedge, without which was a ditch; and between that and the road round the square was a row of very fine elms. That was in July 1814. The twelfth of

The Bank of Ireland, Dublin

August, the centenary of the Hanover accession to the British throne, was to be celebrated with great rejoicings, one part of which was a display of fireworks on Stephen's Green. Having been absent from Dublin upon a visit into the country, from the sixth to the tenth, at my return I observed a most lamentable and sacrilegious havoc which had been made among these trees; they had been stripped almost naked to the trunks, that the fireworks might be the better seen from the houses. To the credit of some of the inhabitants of the square it must be said that there were persons who highly disapproved of the sacrilege, and remonstrated against it: but the order came from authority, and disobedience was not to be thought of.

The following year, when I revisited Dublin, not a tree was left standing. A plan was then almost completed for the improvement and embellishment of the square; the first part of which was to deprive it of its greatest embellishment, these fine trees. I could almost call this an *Irish* way of *embellishing*. Thus much, however, must be confessed, that, such as they had been made in

4

honour of the former twelfth of August, they had almost ceased to be ornamental. For the rest, the square was certainly exceedingly improved; the hedge was removed and the ditch filled up; while instead of them the green was to be enclosed by a handsome iron palisade, and to be laid out with walks and shrubberies after the manner of the squares in London: still I must think that the trees, such as they were when I first saw them, would have given great additional beauty to the whole. There are many very good houses in this square. . .

Near Stephen's Green is Merrion Square, a large area about the dimensions, or perhaps even larger than Portman Square in London. It is modern, and handsomely built: the centre is enclosed with an iron palisade, within which

Sackville Street, Dublin, 1840

St. Stephen's Green, Dublin

shrubs are planted, and beyond them is a gravel walk; the remainder should be a lawn, but when I first saw it the grass had just been cut down for hay. The west side is entirely occupied by the back of Leinster House and the grounds belonging to it. Here again I must observe that in England such a piece of ground would be a fine velvet lawn; in the present instance it was a field where cows and horses were feeding, to which might have been added donkeys, since in one part there was a right noble grove of thistles. . .

Dublin, view from Carlisle Bridge

Dublin's industries, however, in common with those set up along the banks of the canals, never showed any great strength: the city was one of those places which failed to gain much from the progress of the industrial revolution. When the Scottish traveller Henry Inglis visited Dublin in 1834 he found large areas depressed, many thousands on the brink of starvation, and precious little being done to remedy the situation. Inglis was impressed by the magnificent city centre and by the seemingly flourishing state of business therein; but he was shortly to find out that, as he put it himself, 'it is not all gold that glitters'. In his account of his Irish journey, *Ireland in 1834*, he wrote:

FIRST IMPRESSIONS of Dublin are decidedly favourable. Entering from Kingstown, there is little to be seen that is unworthy the approach to a capital; and without passing through any of those wretched suburbs which stretch in many other directions, one is whirled at once into a magnificent centre, where there is an assemblage of all that usually gives evidence of wealth and taste, and of the existence of a great and flourishing city.

A stranger arriving in Dublin in spring, as I did, will be struck even less by the architectural beauty of the city than by other kinds of splendour: I allude to the indulgences of luxury, and the apparent proofs of wealth that are everywhere thrust upon the eye—the numerous private vehicles that fill the streets, and even blockade many of them; the magnificent shops for the sale of articles of luxury and taste, at the doors of which, in Grafton Street, I have counted upwards of twenty handsome equipages; and in certain quarters of the city, the number of splendid houses, and 'legion' of liveried servants. But a little closer observation and more minute inquiry, will in some measure correct these impressions; and will bring to mind the well-known and well-founded proverb that 'it is not all gold that glitters'. . .

In walking through the streets of Dublin, strange and striking contrasts are presented between grandeur and poverty. In Merrion Square, St Stephen's Green and elsewhere, the ragged wretches that are sitting on the steps, contrast strongly with the splendour of the houses and the magnificent equipages that wait without: pass from Merrion Square or Grafton Street, about three o'clock, into what is called the Liberty, and you might easily fancy yourself in another and distant part of Europe. I was extremely struck,

Grattan Bridge and the City Hall, Dublin

the first time I visited the outskirts of the city in the direction of the Phoenix Park, with the strong resemblances to the populations of Spanish towns, which the pauper population of Dublin presented. I saw the same rags, and apparent indolence—the result of a want of employment, and a low state of moral feeling: boys with bare heads and feet, lying on the pavement, whose potato had only to be converted into a melon or a bit of wheaten bread, to make them fit subjects for Murillo; and houses and cottages in a half-ruined state, with paneless windows or no windows at all. I was also struck with the small number of provision shops. In London every fifth or sixth shop is a bacon and cheese-shop. In Dublin, luxuries of a different kind offer their temptations. What would be the use of opening a bacon shop, where the lower orders, who are elsewhere the chief purchasers of bacon, cannot afford to eat bacon, and live upon potatoes?

As I have mentioned the lower orders in Dublin, I may add that from the

8

house in which I lived in Kildare Street, being exactly opposite to the Royal Dublin Society, which was then exhibiting a cattle-show, I was very favourably situated for observing, among the crowd collected, some of those little traits which throw light upon character and condition. I remarked in particular the great eagerness of everyone to get a little employment, and earn a penny or two. I observed another less equivocal proof of low condition. After the cattle had been fed, the half-eaten turnips became the perquisite of the crowd of ragged boys and girls outside. Many and fierce were the scrambles for these precious relics; and a half-gnawed turnip, when once secured, was guarded with the most vigilant jealousy, and was lent for a mouthful to another longing tatterdemalion, as much apparently as an act of extraordinary favour, as if the root had been a pineapple . . .

There was one institution of which I had heard so much that I could not leave Dublin without visiting it. I allude to the Mendicity Society. This Society may be considered a concentration of all the industrious pauperism of Dublin. In a country where there is no legal provision for even the aged and infirm, some institution of this kind is no doubt essential, not only on a principle of humanity, but for common decency's sake. But such institutions are, after all, miserable make-shifts; and a visit to the Dublin Mendicity Society will not put anybody in love with that system of voluntary charity, which, we are told by an eminent divine, is so blessed an encourager of human sympathies.

When I visited the Dublin Mendicity Society, there were 2,145 persons on the charity, of whom two hundred were Protestants. The finances were then at a very low ebb; and the directors of the institution were threatening a procession of the mendicants through the streets, by way of warming the charity of the spectators. This, I understand, has once or twice been resorted to; and I confess, I cannot conceive anything more disgraceful to a civilised community. The English reader, who has never visited Ireland, can have no conception of a spectacle such as this. What a contrast to the gaiety of Grafton Street, would be the filth, and rags, and absolute nakedness, which I saw concentrated in the court of the institution!

The politicians of pre-famine Ireland were, unfortunately, too deeply engrossed in the struggles for Catholic Emancipation and the repeal of the legislative union to pay much attention to poverty, the greatest social ill of the day. Ireland had no Poor Law until 1838 and Henry Inglis's notion of the Irish as a nation of beggars was excusable. It is true that the poor of Dublin were well enough cared for medically: by 1845 there were thirty public hospitals in the city, staffed by some of the most progressive physicians and the most daring surgeons in Europe, including Stokes, Collis, Graves and Crampton, names still familiar to students of medicine. But, unfortunately, illness was the only form of distress for which relief was readily available: the North Dublin Union, when it opened its gates to the hungry masses, could hope to care for only a very small proportion of those who begged for shelter. William Makepeace Thackeray described the Union in his *Irish Sketch Book,* which was published in 1843:

NEAR TO STONEYBATTER lies a group of huge gloomy edifices—an hospital, a penitentiary, a madhouse, and a poorhouse. I visited the latter of these, the North Dublin Union House, an enormous establishment, which accommodates two thousand beggars. Like all the public institutions of the country, it seems to be well-conducted, and is a vast orderly and cleanly place, wherein the prisoners are better clothed, better fed, and better housed than they can hope to be when at liberty. We were taken into all the wards in due order—the schools and nursery for the children; the dining-rooms, day-rooms, etc., of the men and women. Each division is so accommodated, as also with a large court or ground to walk and exercise in . . .

Among the men, there are very few able-bodied, the most of them, the keeper said, having gone out for the harvest time, or as soon as the potatoes came in. If they go out, they cannot return before the expiration of a month: the guardians have been obliged to establish this prohibition, lest the persons requiring relief should go in and out too frequently. The old men were assembled in considerable numbers in a long day-room that is comfortable and warm. Some of them were picking oakum by way of employment; but most of them were past work, all such inmates of the house as are able-bodied being occupied upon the premises. Their hall was airy and as clean as brush and water could make it: the men equally clean, and their grey jackets and Scotch caps stout and warm. Thence we were led, with a sort of satisfaction, by the guardian, to the kitchen—a large room, at the end of which might be seen certain coppers, emitting, it must be owned, a very faint inhospitable smell. It was Friday, and rice-milk is the food on that day, each man being served with a pint-canful, of which cans a great number stood smoking upon stretchers—the platters were laid, each with its portion of salt, in the large clean dining-room hard by. 'Look at that rice,' said the keeper, taking up a bit, 'try it, sir, it's delicious.' I'm sure I hope it is.

The old women's room was crowded with, I should think, at least four hundred old ladies—neat and nice, in white clothes and caps—sitting demurely on benches, doing nothing for the most part; but some employed, like the old men, in fiddling with the oakum. 'There's tobacco here,' says the guardian, in a loud voice, 'who's smoking tobacco?' 'Fait, and I wish dere was some tabacky here,' says an old lady, 'and my service to you, Mr Leary, and I hope one of the gentlemen has a snuff-box, and a pinch for a poor old woman.' But we had no boxes; and if any person who reads this visit, goes to a poor-house or lunatic asylum, let him carry a box, if for that day only—a pinch is like Dives's drop of water to those poor limboed souls. Some of the poor old creatures began to stand up as we came in—I can't say how painful such an honour seemed to me.

There was a separate room for the able-bodied females; and the place and courts were full of stout, red-cheeked, bouncing women. If the old ladies looked respectable, I cannot say the young ones were particularly good-looking; there were some Hogarthian faces amongst them—sly, leering and hideous. I fancied I could see only too well what these girls had been. Is it charitable or not to hope that such bad faces could only belong to bad women?

'Here, sir, is the nursery', said the guide, flinging open the door of a long room. There may have been eighty babies in it, with as many nurses and mothers. Close to the door sat one with as beautiful a face as I almost ever saw: she had at her breast a very sickly and puny child, and looked up, as we entered, with a pair of angelical eyes, and a face that Mr Eastlake could paint— a face that *had* been angelical, that is, for there was the snow still, as it were, but with the footmark on it. I asked her how old she was—she did not know. She could not have been more than fifteen years, the poor child. She said she had been a servant—and there was no need of asking anything more about her. I saw her grinning at one of her comrades as we went out of the room; her face did not look angelical then. Ah, young master or old, young or old

The Great Courtyard, Dublin Castle

villain, who did this: have you not enough wickedness of your own to answer for, that you must take another's sins upon your shoulders; and be this wretched child's sponsor in crime?

. . . But this chapter must be made as short as possible; and so I will not say how much prouder Mr Leary, the keeper, was of his fat pigs than of his paupers—how he pointed us out the burial-ground of the family of the poor—their coffins were quite visible through the niggardly mould; and the children might peep at their fathers over the burial-ground-playground wall . . .

There seems to be a great deal of truth in his friend Charles Lever's assertion that Thackeray's object was simply 'to stroll about the island, see what he can, make a note of it when he gets home, and print the same as soon as may be'. Admittedly, as Lever emphasised, a tourist's vision is a limited one at best;

Thackeray's, however, was very often clouded by his Protestant and imperialistic prejudices, and although his was a kindly nature, when he started moralising he became quite a bore.

Mr and Mrs S. C. Hall showed a much deeper insight into Ireland's problems. Their account of a journey through the country was published in three volumes between 1841 and 1843. The Halls showed none of the religious or class prejudices that are so evident in the accounts of many pre-famine travellers, and if at times they were extraordinarily naive in explaining the causes of Ireland's woes and in suggesting remedies for them, it cannot be said that their opinions were rooted in bigotry. They were conscientious observers of a people they reckoned to be on the brink of doom, even if they were poor political economists.

Anna Maria Hall was born in Dublin in 1800 and was reared in county Wexford. A successful novelist and playwright, she campaigned all through her long life for the alleviation of human distress in all its forms: she fought for women's rights and for London's street musicians, and she is credited with bringing about vast improvements in the poorhouses and hospitals of Britain through the influence of her pen. She married Samuel Carter Hall, a county Waterford man of similar tastes and interests, and their work, *Ireland, Its Scenery and Character,* is the best account of its kind.

When in Dublin Mr and Mrs Hall visited the historic Liberties, situated in the shadow of St Patrick's cathedral:

THERE IS A district in Dublin that possesses many remarkable and peculiar features; it is still called 'the Liberties' —a spacious western tract in the most elevated and airy part of the city. It derives its name from certain privileges and immunities enjoyed by the inhabitants, having manor courts of their own, with seneschals to preside in them; but that of Thomas Court and Donore, is properly confined to the Liberties, and is that from which it takes its name. This court is of very ancient foundation, being held under the charter of King John. It contains within its precincts forty streets and lanes called the Earl of Meath's Liberties, and a population of about forty thousand souls. It has no criminal jurisdiction; but its authority in civil matters, and the amount of sums to be recovered, is unlimited. In all cases under forty shillings the seneschal decides alone; when the sum is greater, he is assisted by a jury. He has a court-house to sit in, and a prison to confine debtors.

The present state of this once flourishing region forms a strong contrast to its former; but it still retains many evidences of what it has been. In passing along its desolate streets, large houses of costly structure everywhere present themselves. Lofty façades adorned with architraves, and mouldings to windows, and door-cases of sculptured stone or marble; grand staircases with carved and gilded balustrades; panelled doors opening into spacious suites of corniced and stuccoed apartments—all attest the opulence of its former inhabitants. They are now the abode only of the most miserable. As they were deserted by the rich, they were filled by the poor; and as they decayed they became the resort of the more abject, who could find no other shelter. So crowded were they at one time, that one hundred and eight persons were found in one house lying on the bare floor, and in one room seven out of twelve were labouring under typhus fever.

It sometimes happens that a sudden stagnation of employment among the poor manufacturers still lingering there causes a pressure of great temporary distress, and then they descend in masses to beg for relief in the lower and more prosperous parts of the city. They resemble an irruption of some strange and foreign horde. A certain wildness of aspect, with pallid faces and squalid persons, at these times, mark the poor artisans of the Liberties as a distinct and separate class from the other inhabitants of the metropolis.

It is singular that the tide of wealthy population in Dublin has taken a contrary direction from that of London. They have deserted the high, airy, and salubrious site at the west end, which is now desolate, and selected the flats and swamps of the east. Thus, by a strange perversion of taste, the elevated site and wholesome air are left to the poor, while the rich have emigrated into the unwholesome morass.

Not content with offering their own opinions on the condition of the country, the Halls jotted down, accurately they assure us, the comments of the poor on various aspects of life. They eavesdropped in the halls of the courts of justice, they listened to the complaints of destitute families as they were being evicted from their cabins, they interviewed out-of-work craftsmen in their homes. In the Liberties of Dublin they spoke to a poor weaver whose wife had recently died:

'SHE WAS FROM the country,' continued the poor man, whose heart was evidently full of the one subject, 'and the day I married her she was just sixteen, and had never been near a town, or seen a soldier, only spent her days in the open fields, haymaking and milking, and tending her uncle's sheep. He was a man well to do, and she was the eldest of five orphans, that he brought up with his own sister's children, poor things, and he made no differ in them, only she loved me, poor girl, and I told her, with all the courage I had, that Dublin was a dark place for the poor. She laughed at that, and 'deed I've since thought she did not know what darkness was—*then*; anyhow, I had a better room to bring her to than this, though this is not bad; it's a palace to many. She was so lighthearted, she made every place lightsome; but I remember how seriously she asked me one day, if "the sun ever shone in Dublin". It is not to say she never gave me an uneasy word; but she never gave me one that wasn't a blessing; even when I took a drop too much of a Monday she'd strive to make me at peace with myself, while she'd wind round to the moral of everything, so that I might not do it again. No one ever said she was a beauty, yet I never looked off my work into her face that I didn't think her an angel. Somehow

The Rotunda, Dublin

she never throve here, though she lingered with me for eight years, poor girl! She'd smile and shake her head when they called this 'the Liberty'. She had some notion, when I told her I lived in the Liberty of the city of Dublin, that it was a fresh, country sort of place; she had more innocent turns in her head than her own child. Why, she'd burst out crying at a handful of daisies, and keep the bit of bread out of her own mouth to buy a halfpenny bunch of primroses. But I beg your honour's pardon', continued the poor weaver, 'only when I think of her my heart seems so full that I'm thankful to any one that'll listen to me'.

We observed that the frame of his loom was stuck over in many places with ballads; indeed we have seldom entered a weaver's room without perceiving a similar display; and the songs so fixed are generally pretty sure indexes to the opinions of the owners. In Dublin such scraps were chiefly political . . .

The Halls also remarked on the curious rigidity of the class-structure of pre-famine Ireland. The aristocracy of wealth had, as yet, made little way; and to be of 'good family' was a surer introduction to society, than to be of large fortune. The prejudice in favour of 'birth', the Halls tell us, was almost universal, and pervaded all ranks:

HENCE ARISES that perpetual straining after a higher station, to which many worthy families have been sacrificed: persons in business rarely persevere until they have amassed fortunes, but retire as early as possible after they have acquired competence; and the subdivisions which their properties necessarily undergo, when junior branches are to be provided for, create a numerous class, almost peculiar to Ireland, of young men possessing the means of barely living without labour, disdaining the notion of 'turning to trade', unable to acquire professions, and ill-suited to adorn them if obtained; content to drag on existence in a state of miserable and degrading dependence, doing nothing—literally, 'too proud to work, but not ashamed to beg'. This feeling operates upon the various grades of society; and the number of 'idlers' in the busy world is fearfully large; from 'the walking gentleman' of the upper ranks, to the 'half-sir' of the middle, and 'the Jackeen' of the class a little above the lower; the 'walking gentleman' being always elegantly attired, of course always unemployed, with ample leisure for the studies which originate depravity; the 'half-sir' being, generally, a younger brother, with little or no income of his own, and so educated as to be deprived, utterly, of the energy and self-dependence which create usefulness; the 'Masther Tom', who broke the dogs, shot the crows, first backed the vicious horse, and, followed by a half-pointer, half-lurcher, poached, secretly, upon his elder brother's land, but more openly upon the lands of his neighbours; the 'Jackeen' being a production found everywhere, but most abundantly in large towns. Happily, however, the class is not upon the increase. The 'Jackeen' might have been seen—regularly a few years ago, and now occasionally—at early morning lounging against the college rails, with the half-intoxicated, half-insolent air that betokens a night passed in debauch; his stockings, that had once been white, falling from under the drab-green, ill-fitting trousers over the shoes; his coat usually of green; his waistcoat of some worn and faded finery; and the segment of collar that peeped above the stock, fashionable in cut, but not in quality, was crushed and degraded from its original property; his hat, always a little on one side, had a knowing 'bend' over the right eye; one of his arms was passed, with that peculiar affectation of carelessness which evinces care, through the rails, and brought round, so as to enable the hand to shift the coarse and bad cigar that rested on his lip—there was a torn glove upon the other; and his dull bloodshot eyes winked impudently upon every girl that passed.

Donnybrook Fair, held a few miles from the centre of Dublin, was a major tourist attraction in the early years of the century. The celebrated German rake, Prince Hermann Ludwig Heinrich Von Puckler-Muskau, visited the fair in 1828. The Prince tended to over-emphasise the rakish aspects of Irish life. A great lover of wine and women, he himself lived life to the full. He was sent to Leipzig university to study law but gave it up to join the Saxon army. Soon he forsook soldiering to avoid being arrested for debt, and began his European travels. When the Napoleonic wars started, however, he rejoined the army and eventually found himself military commander of Bruges. After the wars he settled down on one of the family estates and in 1817 married Lucie, Countess of Pappenheim, daughter of the chancellor of state. Nine years later he divorced Lucie and set off on his travels again, looking

Donnybrook Fair

for a richer wife. He became the friend of Goethe and Mehemet Ali, and he was a welcome guest in most of the royal houses of Europe. He died in 1871 at the ripe old age of eighty-six.

In his account of his Irish travels he displayed a warm humanity. He contributed to O'Connell's campaign funds and he never failed to lash those he held responsible for the squalor he saw everywhere he went in Ireland—the British government, the absentee landlords and the established Church.

Here is his account of the fair held at Donnybrook the year before O'Connell won emancipation:

I RODE OUT again today for the first time to see the fair at Donnybrook, near Dublin, which is a kind of popular festival. Nothing indeed can be more national! The poverty, the dirt, and the wild tumult were as great as the glee and merriment with which the cheapest pleasures were enjoyed. I saw things eaten and drunk with delight, which forced me to turn my head quickly away to remain master of my disgust. Heat and dust, crowd and stench, (*il faut le dire*), made it impossible to stay long: but these do not annoy the natives. There were many hundred tents, all ragged like the people, and adorned with tawdry rags instead of flags; many contented themselves with a cross on a hoop; one had hoisted a dead and half-putrid cat as a sign! The lowest sort of rope-dancers and posture-masters exercised their toilsome vocation on stages of planks, and dressed in shabby finery, dancing and grimacing in the dreadful heat till they were completely exhausted. A third part of the public lay, or rather rolled about, drunk; others ate, screamed, shouted and fought. The women rode about, sitting two and three upon an ass, pushed their way through the crowd, smoked with great delight, and coquetted with their sweethearts. The most ridiculous group was one which I should have thought indigenous only to Rio de la Plata: two beggars were seated on a horse, who by his wretched plight, seemed to supplicate for them; they had no saddle, and a piece of twine served as reins. As I left the fair, a pair of lovers, excessively drunk, took the same road. It was a rich treat to watch their behaviour. Both were horribly ugly, but treated each other with the greatest tenderness, and the most delicate attention. The lover especially displayed a sort of chivalrous politeness. Nothing could be more gallant, and at the same time more respectful, than his repeated efforts to preserve his fair one from falling, although he had no little difficulty in keeping his own balance. From his ingratiating demeanour and her delighted smiles, I could also perceive that he was using every endeavour to entertain her agreeably; and that her answers, notwithstanding her *exalté* state, were given with a coquetry and an air of affectionate intimacy which would have been exquisitely becoming and attractive in a pretty woman.

My reverence for truth compels me to add that not the slightest trace of

19

English brutality was to be perceived: they were more like French people, though their gaiety was mingled with more humour, and more genuine good-nature; both of which are national traits of the Irish, and are always doubled by poteen (the best sort of whiskey illicitly distilled).

Don't reproach me for the vulgarity of the pictures I send you: they are more akin to nature than the painted dolls of our salons.

THE PROVINCIAL TOWNS

THIRTY coach roads and two canals radiated from Dublin by 1845, giving the travellers access to many of the country's main towns. The coach roads were well-built and well-maintained, and the travellers found that a journey on the Irish roads was much more comfortable than one on the roads of England or France. But a seat behind the coachman, or on one of the canal boats, lacked the comforts of the railway carriage, and in 1845, much to the travellers' regret, Ireland could boast of only eighty-five miles of railway tracks.

The fastest growing town in pre-famine Ireland was Belfast. At the beginning of the century its population was approximately nineteen thousand; by 1850 it was in the region of one hundred thousand. It was the economic centre of the rich Lagan valley, the marketing town of the Ulster linen industry which had flourished in the cottage homes of the sturdy planter stock. Belfast had prospered under the union, and Henry Inglis was very impressed by it when he first saw it in 1834:

IT NEEDS BUT a glance at Belfast and the surrounding country to perceive that this town, and its neighbouring districts, have nothing in common with the rest of Ireland. It is true that Londonderry, Coleraine, and the other northern towns and districts, do not present a contrast to Belfast; the perfect contrasts must be looked for in Leinster, Munster and Connaught: but the visual evidences of prosperity are so much more abundant, and so much more striking in Belfast, than

even in the other most flourishing towns of Ulster, that I am justified in
saying that Belfast has little or nothing in common with the rest of Ireland.
Within the town, and without the town, the proofs of prosperity are equally
striking. Walk towards the outskirts, and fine broad streets, and handsome
rows and squares, evidently but of yesterday and as evidently the residences
of wealthy persons, are seen stretching in all directions, from the central part
of the town: return into the commercial part of the town, and nothing will
be seen that might not justify a comparison with the most flourishing among
the manufacturing and commercial cities of the Empire. Walk into the
neighbouring country, and the evidences of enterprise and capital are still
more abundant. On all sides are seen, near and far, manufactories, or mills,
as they are called, of immense extent, evidently newly erected, and vying—
nay, I think, surpassing—in size, and in all other respects, the mills and

The departure of the Limerick coach

factories of our great manufacturing towns; others are seen in course of erection; and, round and round, scores of tall chimneys, and their clouds of utilitarian smoke, remind one of Manchester, Glasgow and Leeds. No mud cabins—these I had left behind me long ago—no poor cottages form a suburb, or disfigure it; and neither in the streets, nor in the suburbs, is the eye arrested by objects of compassion. There is, in fact, no trace of an Irish population among any class: the lower orders are not ragged, and starving, and idle, because unemployed; the middle and upper classes are not loungers and men of pleasure. Pleasure, in Belfast, is a very secondary consideration. No town, perhaps, of the United Kingdom contains so few who live upon a fixed income, derived from capital or property. Every one has something to do; and every one appears to find pleasure in doing something. Tradesmen do not here shut up shop, and set up for fine gentlemen, on the strength of a few thousand pounds. Merchants do not ingeniously mingle the *utile* and the *dulce*. Business is life here—and life is business: and the merchant, worth £50,000, looks upon it as a sufficient relaxation from the toils of the Linenhall, that he spends the evening at his country house, and regales his eye with a view of his well-tilled bleach-fields. It is impossible that Cork, Limerick, or Waterford, should ever become altogether like Belfast; because the character of the Scotch and the Irish is essentially different . . .

The establishments of the merchants in the Linenhall, are well worth a visit; the linen made up for the market is really a pretty sight to one who never saw it before, bound round with its embossed gilt paper, and gaudy ribbons. The expense of ornamenting the linen increases the price to the purchaser from a penny to a penny-halfpenny a yard; but in the American market, they would not look at the linen unless it were so ornamented. One would not expect this of sturdy republicans . . . The linen trade is of that peculiar character, that the labour of young and old, boys and girls, is required: and although the weaver earns but eight shillings per week, he has perhaps two girls who earn six shillings between them on the spinning wheel; and a boy or two, who earn three shillings or four shillings apiece in the bleach field . . .

From the details which I have given, it may be gathered that there is little complaint of want of employment in Belfast and its neighbourhood. The sources of employment are many. The export trade, and the extensive bacon and provision yards connected with it, are one important source of

Above
The Linenhall, Belfast

Left
Buying China, from a
painting by Erskine Nicol

employment. The shipping and ship-building, also connected with it, employ many. Of the linen trade, as the most fertile of all sources of employment, I have already spoken at sufficient length. To this must be added, as other sources of employment, the calico and muslin trade. I have also mentioned the domestic manufacture of tools and utensils employed in these manufactures: to all these sources of employment must be added the demand for mason and carpenter work, and common labour, in so improving a town: together with the porterage and other labour required, in a town to and from which between seventy and eighty public conveyances run daily. Altogether there is nearly full and constant employment for labour in Belfast. I visited many of the houses of the lower class, in the suburbs and lanes of the town, and found no complaint of want of work: and I am inclined to think that all the healthy and industrious labourers can afford to live in tolerable comfort. I know that labourers could with difficulty be found when I was at Belfast; and the ordinary rate of wages was then 1s. 3d. per day. The number of infirm and diseased poor in Belfast bears no comparison with the infirm pauper population of Limerick. In a city where there is no employment for the people, there must be a constant increase in the number of diseased and infirm; since a few weeks of privation, and imperfect and unwholesome nourishment, or even a day or two of abstinence, will reduce the strongest, able-bodied labourer to the condition of an infirm pauper, and lay him on a sick bed. And besides, no large quarter of Belfast is the property of a Lord Limerick.

The middle classes of Belfast are not only a thinking, but an educated, and a reading people. There are no fewer than fourteen booksellers in Belfast; and all of them enjoy a fair share of business. Nor are libraries wanting. The Linenhall library contains about nine thousand volumes; the town contains four circulating libraries, and more than one private book society. . . .

The population of Belfast is divided into many religious sects. The most numerous sect is the Presbyterian and its dissenters; the Catholics come next; then the Church; and then the Methodists. Besides these, there are of course smaller sects, such as Baptists, Unitarians, etc. The increase in the Catholic population of Belfast has been great of late years. Sixty years ago, the number of Catholics did not reach sixty families; twenty years ago their number amounted to about four thousand; and at present the Catholic population reaches fifteen thousand. This is no real increase of Popery. The whole population twenty years ago was about half what it is at present; and although the Catholic population has trebled itself since that time, this is only a result of the rapid increase of the town in prosperity, by which labour has been attracted from the country.

I have already spoken of the distinctive character of the people of the north. Nowhere is this seen more clearly than in Belfast. Even among the richest merchants and manufacturers, many of whom are worth fifty thousand pounds and some perhaps double that sum, no display is seen; no pomp, or ostentation. Things are plain, but comfortable; and although there is no want of courtesy, and attention to strangers who are well recommended, the hospitalities of Belfast are not offered with that *empressement* which distinguishes the south and west. The people of Belfast count the cost of everything; and to this disposition the Belfast merchant owes, in a great measure, the possession of those means of enterprise and liberality, which are shewn in his own private speculations, as well as in the public benefits for which the town is indebted to him. The merchants of Belfast are too busy, and too much occupied in money getting, to have time for much company keeping; and Sunday, which in the south and west, is a day of pleasure, is here passed at church and meeting houses.

Despite Henry Inglis's assertions to the contrary, great poverty did exist in certain sectors of Belfast in 1834. Certainly squalor and destitution on the scale he witnessed in the south didn't exist there, but the Poor Law of 1838 was greeted with relief in Belfast as well as in Dublin, Cork and Limerick. Sir Walter Scott, on his way to Belfast in 1825, noticed 'mountainous packages of old clothes: the cast-off raiment of the Scotch beggars on its way to a land where beggary is the staple of life'. His biographer, Lockhart, remarked that Sir Walter rather irritated a military passenger, a stout old Highlander, by asking whether it had ever occurred to him that the beautiful checkery of the clan tartans might have originated in a pious wish, on the part of the Scottish Gael, to imitate the tatters of the parent race. In Belfast Scott and Lockhart saw the use of the imported rags:

ONE MAN, APPARENTLY happy and gay, returning to his work from breakfast, with pipe in mouth, had a coat of

26

which I do not believe any three inches together were of the same colour, yea, or stuff—red, black, yellow; cloth, velveteen, corduroy—the complete image of a tattered coverlid, originally made, on purpose, of particularly small patches; no shirt, and almost no breeches; yet this is the best part of Ireland and the best population. What shall we see in the south?

This is what Pückler-Muskau saw in the town of Athenry, in county Galway, a few years later.

THIS BATHING PLACE, Athenry, is one of the curiosities of Ireland. No Polish village can have a more wretched aspect. The cluster of cabins is on a bare hill rising out of the bog, without tree or bush, without an inn, without any convenience, inhabited only by ragged beggars, and by the few invalids who bring with them everything they want, and must send for even the most trifling article of food to Galway, a distance of twelve miles. Once it was otherwise; and it saddens one to see

A village in the west of Ireland, 1847

at the further extremity of this wretched village the proud ruins of better times. Here stood a rich abbey, now overgrown with ivy; the arches which once protected the sanctuary lie in fragments amid the unsheltered altars and tombstones. Further on is a castle with walls ten feet thick, in which King John held his court of justice when he came over to Ireland.

I visited these ruins with a most numerous company: I do not exaggerate when I say that at least two hundred half-naked beings, two-thirds of whom were children, had collected round my carriage at a very early hour in the morning, doing nothing: they now thronged round me, all begging, and shouting, 'Long life to your honour!' Every individual among them stuck faithfully by me, leaping over stones and brambles. The strangest compliment now and then resounded from the midst of the crowd: at last some called out, 'Long life to the King!' On my return I threw two or three handfuls of copper among them; and in a minute half of them, old and young, lay prostrate in the sand, while the others ran with all speed into a whiskey shop, fighting furiously all the way.

Such is Ireland! Neglected or oppressed by the Government, debased by the stupid intolerance of the English priesthood, and marked by poverty and the poison of whiskey, for the abode of naked beggars!

Many of the tourists commented on the total lack of interest shown by the town councils in the plight of the poor. New Ross in county Wexford which had built up a thriving trade with Newfoundland and continental Europe in the previous century was, according to Atkinson, an Englishman who visited the place in 1815, a shining example to the rest of Ireland in the matter of private and public charity. Atkinson wrote:

. . . THE SICK POOR institution, fever hospital and dispensary, a light airy edifice, which commands an agreeable view over the town to the river and surrounding country, was founded in the year 1809 and endowed with a perpetual annuity of three hundred pounds by the late Mrs Haughton Bolger, since which period 4,297 persons have been taken under care, and of these, as the treasurer informed me, 4,145 had been discharged cured or considerably relieved. The house contains two sick and two convalescent wards, each adapted to the accommodation of four patients, and if we may judge of the management of this house by its convenience, cleanliness, and purity of air, as well as by the effects we have noticed, we may well pronounce this establishment a public blessing to the neighbourhood, but the funds (comprising the above legacy, an annual grant from the grand jury, and annual and weekly subscriptions, amounting in the whole to upwards of seven hundred pounds per annum) relieve by much a larger number of the weak and infirm poor of Ross, as extern patients, than those who are the proper subjects of the charity of the hospital.

Beside those public buildings, which on the ground of ornament more directly attract the attention of a stranger, the following charitable institutions and schools for education deserve to be noticed, in an estimate of the improvements of the place. The principal charitable school, which comprises apartments for the education of youth of both sexes, is organised on the Lancasterian system, supported by voluntary subscription, and conducted committee. Instruction is administered here without religious distinction, and to prevent the jealousies resulting from which, (not among the children, but in the minds of those who have an interest in their principles) neither creed nor

St Patrick's Bridge, Cork, drawn by Thomas Creswick

Waterford City, 1843

catechism is introduced, but there is a poor school in the town, conducted by certain Roman Catholic clergymen, where the peculiar tenets of that church are, of course, carefully inculcated.

The lying-in hospital comes next in order—it receives and accommodates, during their confinement, six poor women at a time, whose uncomfortable domestic circumstances at such a period render them proper objects of this charity. This institution, founded in 1809, and supported chiefly by the subscriptions of the inhabitants, has admitted within the pale of its benefits, seventy-eight poor women since the period of its foundation.

There is also a charitable repository, opened in 1805, for the purpose of supplying poor married women at their own lodgings, with suitable comforts, medical aid and attendance, during their confinement in child-bed, and to

30

provide clothing for their infants. This little charity is chiefly supported by profits on the sale of works of ladies who are friends to the institution, and by the sale of presents made thereto; and in connection with the lying-in hospital is solely indebted to the ladies of the town for its continuance and support. It has been the instrument of relieving five hundred and eighty women and their children since its foundation.

Trinity hospital is another charitable institution of this place—it was endowed by a gentleman by the name of Dormer, and supports fourteen widows, each of whom has the use, during life, of two apartments, and an income of about twenty pounds per annum.

A charitable loan instituted in 1801, for lending out small sums free of interest to tradesmen and others, is deserving a note of observation in this estimate. The money constituting this fund is distributed in sums not exceeding five, and not less than one guinea to each, and is repaid by weekly instalments, at the rate of sixpence halfpenny per week, for each guinea lent.

Galway city, the capital of the west, was in a poor way when Dr James Johnson, sometime physician to William IV, first saw the place in 1844:

THE HUGE LOUGH CORRIB discharges its pellucid waters through Galway in a foaming torrent that would turn all the mills and spinning-jennies in Manchester! But, alas! this gigantic 'water-power' is turned to little other account than that of revolving the wheels of two or three flour mills, and washing the linen of the Galwegians and fishermen of the Claddagh! The river here rushes into the bay, clear and rapid as the 'blue and arrowy Rhone' at Geneva: I would that the citizens could employ such a willing and able engine in the various operations to which the Genevese direct their beautiful stream! In Galway, unfortunately, there are more monasteries than mills—more monks than manufacturers—more nuns than cotton-spinners—more friars than hand-loom weavers—more con-fessionals for cleansing the soul than factories for clothing the body.

Like many another traveller, Dr Johnson was fascinated by the fishing village

31

The Claddagh, Galway, drawn by John Leech

of the Claddagh, on Galway's outskirts. 'Wild, fierce and original', Thackeray
had called the place, and Johnson agreed with him.

HERE WE HAVE a kind of Indian caste,
located in the vicinity of an Iberian colony—a community of some six
thousand fishers—men, women, and children, all living by or on fish—
marrying and inter-marrying only among their own caste, and rarely if ever
intermixing with their neighbouring Iberians, except to sell their finny
produce or purchase materials for catching more! There cannot be a doubt
that this exclusion from society, and this ban against the infusion of strange
and fresh blood from without, will one day so deteriorate the race, that a
monstrous hybrid progeny will appear in the Bay of Galway!

. . . Passing the bridge over the noisy river that flows from Lough Corrib,
I directed my steps to the Claddagh, and explored every street and lane in

32

that singular colony. The Claddagh is certainly entitled to the epithets, 'wild, fierce, and original'. They have a king of their own, though I could see nothing like a palace or a court. They are also governed by laws of their own making—sanctioned, of course, by their sovereign.

While rambling through this great mass of wretched huts, and apparent community of beggars, my ears were saluted by music and merrymaking, and, on approaching the spot, I found that a 'dignity ball' was going on, to which I was politely invited by one of the masters of the ceremonies at the door. The ball-room was about eighteen or twenty feet square, without any seats or furniture—and the light was admitted through the chimney, the door, and one window without glass. There might be fifty or sixty people in this place, all squatted on the ground, except the dancers. There was just light enough to discern dimly, the features and costume of this motley assemblage, and so strange a group I never before beheld . . .

· I understood that the queen and some of the princesses were performing at this dignity ball; but that the king and prince royal were at market, selling their fish, a grand haul of which they had taken the preceding day. On quitting the ball-room I again perambulated the whole of the Claddagh, and entered into a great number of their wigwams. I found that the inhabitants were not so wretched and impoverished as the exteriors of their huts indicated. It is an advantage common to all fishing-towns and villages, that the women and children are furnished with more means of industry and employment, connected with the avocations of the men, than in any other places. The consequences are, that the youngsters, of both sexes, can afford to marry younger, and are able to bring up a family easier, than the labourers or artisans of any other class. The Claddagh offers no exception to this rule. On the contrary, every hut is swarming with women and children, all, except the infants, employed in some manner or other, connected with the fishery.

I cannot take leave of this singular community, without recommending it to the attention of the Liberator and the whole of the Repealers. It is the very beau ideal—the very model of a *limited monarchy*, with its 'domestic legislature'—its resident court, resident aristocracy, resident gentry—and, to crown all, its 'fixity of tenure'! I do not believe that there has been a single *ejectment* there, except by the hand of death, in the memory of man. But the kingdom of Claddagh possesses many negative as well as *positive* advantages. There is here no '*driving*' for rent; for there are no cattle to drive—no seizures

33

of live-stock, except of such as it would be very difficult to catch, and, if caught, would not have a singular purchaser; no middlemen or rack-renters; no Bastilles; for each cabin is a *poor*-house, and supports its own paupers.

Then the state expenses are on so moderate a scale, that they would ensure the approbation of Joseph Hume himself. Thus the king rarely indulges in any other sport than that of fishing—and on his return, either he or the queen carries the fish to market, for the good of the court establishment. The royal family indeed set a pattern of industry and economy to their subjects. They spin the thread, construct the nets, and darn the stockings for the sovereign; and never ask a shilling from the community on the birth of a prince or princess!

Cork city had a population of approximately 81,000 when Thackeray visited it in the early forties. Agricultural produce was the basis of whatever prosperity it could boast of; there were bacon-curing factories and bacon, butter and pork depots. The city was one of the main provisioning centres for the British navy. This is part of Thackeray's account of it:

AMIDST THE BUSTLE and gaieties of the agricultural meeting, the working-day aspect of the city was not to be judged of: but I passed a fortnight in the place afterwards, during which time it settled down to its calm and usual condition. The flashy French and plated-goods shops, which made a show for the occasion of the meeting, disappeared; you were no longer crowded and jostled by smart male and female dandies in walking down Patrick Street or the Mall: the poor little theatre had scarcely a soul in its bare benches; I went once, but the dreadful brass-band of a dragoon regiment blew me out of doors. This music could be heard much more pleasantly at some distance off in the street.

One sees in this country many a grand and tall iron gate leading into a very shabby field covered with thistles; and the simile of the gate will in some degree apply to this famous city of Cork, which is certainly not a city of palaces, but of which the outlets are magnificent. That towards Killarney leads by the Lee—the old avenue of Mardyke, and the rich green pastures stretching down to the river—and as you pass by the portico of the county-gaol, as fine and as glancing as a palace, you see the wooded heights on the other side of the fair stream, crowded with a thousand pretty villas and terraces, presenting every image of comfort and prosperity.

Along the quays up to Saint Patrick's bridge there is a certain bustle. Some forty ships may be lying at anchor along the walls of the quay: and its pavements are covered with goods of various merchandise; here a cargo of hides; yonder a company of soldiers, their kits, and their Dollies, who are taking leave of the red-coats at the steamer's side. Then you shall see a fine squeaking, shrieking drove of pigs embarking by the same conveyance, and insinuated into the steamer by all sorts of coaxing, threatening, and wheedling. Seamen are singing and yeehoing on board; grimy colliers smoking at the liquor-shops along the quay; and as for the bridge—there is a crowd of idlers on that, you may be sure, sprawling over the balustrade for ever and ever, with long ragged coats, steeple hats, and stumpy doodeens.

Then along the coal-quay you may see a clump of jingle-drivers, who have all a word for your honour; and in Patrick Street, at three o'clock, when 'the Rakes of Mallow' gets under weigh (a cracked old coach with the paint rubbed off, some smart horses, and an exceedingly dingy harness)—at three o'clock, you will be sure to see at least forty persons waiting to witness the departure of the said coach; so that the neighbourhood of the inn has an air of some bustle.

At the other extremity of the town, if it be assize time, you will see some five hundred persons squatting in the court-house, or buzzing and talking within; the rest of the respectable quarter of the city is pretty free from anything like bustle. There is no more life in Patrick Street than in Russell Square of a sunshiny day; and as for the Mall, it is as lonely as the chief street of a German Residenz . . .

Not far from the quays is an open space where the poor hold a market or bazaar. Here is liveliness and business enough; ragged boys gloating over dirty apple and pie-stalls; fish frying, and raw and stinking; clothes-booths, where you might buy a wardrobe for scarecrows; old nails, hoops, bottles, and marine wares; old battered furniture, that has been sold against starvation. In the streets round about this place, on a sunshiny day, all the black gaping windows and mouldy steps are covered with squatting lazy figures—women, with bare breasts, nursing babies, and leering a joke as you pass by—ragged children paddling everywhere. It is but two minutes' walk out of Patrick

35

Blackpool, Cork, drawn by T. C. Croker

Street, where you come upon . . . a grand French emporium of dolls, walking-sticks, carpet-bags and perfumery. The markets hard by have a rough, old-fashioned, cheerful look; it's a comfort after the misery to hear a red butcher's wife crying after you to buy an honest piece of meat . . .

I think, in walking the streets and looking at the ragged urchins crowding there, every Englishman must remark that the superiority of intelligence is here, and not with us. I never saw such a collection of bright-eyed, wild, clever, eager faces. Mr Maclise has carried away a number of them in his memory; and the lovers of his admirable pictures will find more than one Munster countenance under a helmet in company of Macbeth, or in a slashed doublet alongside of Prince Hamlet, or in the very midst of Spain in company with Signor Gil Blas. Gil Blas himself came from Cork, and not from Oviedo . . .

In the midst of your pleasure, three beggars have hobbled up, and are howling supplications to the Lord. One is old and blind, and so diseased and hideous, that straightway all the pleasure of the sight round about vanishes from you—that livid ghastly face interposing between you and it. And so it is throughout the south and west of Ireland, the traveller is haunted by the face of the popular starvation. It is not the exception, it is the condition of the people. In this fairest and richest of countries, men are suffering and starving by millions. There are thousands of them at this minute stretched in the sunshine at their cabin doors with no work, scarcely any food, no hope seemingly. Strong countrymen are lying in bed 'for the hunger'—because a man lying on his back does not need so much food as a person a-foot. Many of them have torn up the unripe potatoes from their little gardens, to exist now, and must look to winter, when they shall have to suffer starvation and cold too. The epicurean, and traveller for pleasure, had better travel anywhere than here; where there are miseries that one does not dare to think of; where one is always feeling how helpless pity is, and how hopeless relief, and is perpetually made ashamed of being happy.

The Ireland that most interested the pre-famine tourists, however, was not the Ireland of a decaying town. 'The real Ireland is rural Ireland', said Philip Hardy in 1827. 'This is the Ireland of a starving tenantry of whom a million or more still cherish their ancient language and literature; this is the Ireland of the absentee landlord and of the tithe proctor; this is the land of faction fights, of fairs, races and patrons.'

It was an Ireland about which most of the travellers who came to visit it sounded an apocalyptic note.

RURAL IRELAND

To THE vast majority of the people of rural Ireland the Union must have seemed rather irrelevant. Their immediate problem was one of survival and their ballad makers sang of tithe proctors and landlords rather than about those who had favoured the legislative union.

> *Their good, ill, health, joy or discontent,*
> *Being end, aim, religion, rent, rent, rent.*
>
> Byron

Rural Irish society was a complex one, and the condition of its various strata depended on the hold each particular class had on the land. At the top of the social structure there were the landlords and on their attitudes depended the condition of the tenant farmers. Many of the absentee landlords were interested only in exacting as high a rent as possible from as many tenants as possible; others who lived on their estates were themselves impoverished and could do little to help their tenants.

A tenant's hold on his farm depended on whether or not he could pay his rent, which could be raised at will by the landlord in cases where the tenant had no lease. In many districts, in the south and west in particular, the farmers' holdings were small; in pre-famine Ireland more than eighty per cent of the holdings were under fifteen acres and almost fifty per cent were of less than five acres. The smaller farmers were usually obliged to sell all their produce, with the exception of the potato crop, to pay their rents, and their living conditions differed little from those of the agricultural labourers.

38

The latter lived in a cabin built on a plot in which he grew his potatoes. He worked his rent, as the saying went: he received no money wages as these were balanced against his rent. He had, at least, a guarantee of constant employment.

The rest of the rural population had no land and no constant employment, but they often took land on conacre. The man who depended on this arrangement for a livelihood was constantly in danger of starvation. The rents were high (often as high as ten pounds an Irish acre) and it was no wonder that, as Lady Chatterton observed in 1838 during her progress through the land, 'their prayers are seldom offered for any heavenly favours other than God's blessing on the potato crop'.

Raithe an ocrais (the hungry season) the landless labourers of west Cork

Women digging potatoes in county Roscommon

used to call the summer months when the supply of potatoes had been used up and the new crop was not yet ready to dig. During this time many of the labourers from the poorer districts were obliged to leave their families and seek work in more prosperous areas. While the labourers of west Cork and Kerry moved to Tipperary and Limerick and those of Galway and Mayo went looking for employment in the midlands, their wives and children often took to the road and lived by begging.

These conditions were aggravated by an economic crisis brought about by a rapid increase in population. Between the time of the Union and 1841 the population rose from approximately five million to 8,175,000, and the majority depended on the land for a living. In many districts holdings were divided and subdivided to provide a potato patch and a site for a cabin; parishes of cabin dwellers living on the verge of destitution was the result. This great evil of subdivision could only lead to disaster. To remedy it meant mass evictions, and those freewheeling landlords who allowed it to go on were far more popular than those who attempted to halt it by any means, fair or foul.

For the best part of twenty years after the Union, the country was administered under coercive legislation. Agrarian secret societies flourished, combating terror of one kind with terror of another; but the only land acts passed at the time were drafted, not for the benefit of the tenants, but to simplify the process of eviction for the landlords.

'Crawling slaves' Daniel O'Connell called the Irish of his day. Certainly John Gough, who toured the country in 1814, would not have disagreed with O'Connell's opinion of many of the poor people he led. Writing about the labourers in the vicinity of Cahir, county Tipperary, Gough remarked:

THE GENERAL condition of the labouring people, in this and the neighbouring counties, is certainly very wretched, seldom treated by their employers with that humanity and attention their useful labours so justly merit. A cabin and an acre of ground, generally held at fifty shillings per annum, under an obligation of working for the farmer at sixpence per day, form their chief means of subsistence. On these slender resources, the labourer has often to provide for a wife and half a dozen children, who have no employment till they approach the age of puberty.

The wife procures a little in some parts of the country, by spinning flax or wool, in others knitting, and in a few places by occasional labour in the fields.

But poverty is not all these poor people have to bear. They have to encounter insults much harder to endure than poverty. It has been the policy of their imperious masters, to keep them totally ignorant of the blessings of our glorious constitution, the beauty of which is carefully hid from their eyes. They have no idea of an impartial administration of justice, and should they have a dispute with any of their equals (for to contend with their superiors never enters their heads) they would not think of any dependence on the justice of their cause, but on the interest, that through the means of their master, or any other gentleman, could be made with the justice of the peace. If a man on horseback, riding in dirty weather, should meet a poor man on foot, who did not immediately get out of his way, to let him pass easily on, he would give him a pretty good chastisement with his horse whip, and the peasant would not offer to resist, but with hat in hand, ask his pardon. Of this I have been myself an eye-witness. And I was credibly informed, when in Clonmel, that about thirty years ago, there lived a very hospitable

A cabin on the Duke of Leinster's estate, 1843

and generous kind of a gentleman, in that neighbourhood, who had an estate of about two thousand pounds a year, (I think his name was Magrath), who, when riding along the road, if he chanced to meet or overtake a labourer or tradesman, who happened to be singing or whistling, and did not instantly cease in respect to the gentleman as he passed, or neglected voluntarily to take off his hat, immediately the great man would descend from his horse, and either, in person, use his whip pretty plentifully on the carcase of the delinquent, or cause the punishment to be inflicted by his servant. Now, when such a case as this occurred, if the poor man aggrieved happened to know that his punishment was illegal, and should endeavour to obtain legal redress, it would be a difficult matter for him to find a justice of peace that would take his examination, and should he make the attempt, he might think himself well off to escape another horsewhipping for his presumption . . .

The *Ulster Custom* left the tenants in Ulster in a much better position than those in the other provinces. It was a practice or usage by which a tenant paying rent to his landlord should not be evicted without being paid by the incoming tenant, or by the landlord, the full marketable price of his interest in the farm, this interest being the value of his own improvements, and those inherited from his ancestors. This custom ensured that the landlord could not raise the rent as the tenant effected improvements on his holding. The tenant benefited from his own efforts, and this encouraged him to be hardworking and law-abiding; the result was to be seen in the comparatively high standard of living in Ulster. In John Gough's time, tenant right, as the tenant's interest was called, was selling at from five to thirty pounds per acre. But this right depended on the Ulster Custom; it was not a legal right, and was not liked by the landlords, and the tenants frequently banded together to protect it. John Gough had this to say about the Ulster tenants:

HOW VERY DIFFERENT is the situation of the common people in Ulster province, though living under the same government, and subject to the very same laws. There, the poorest man, looking upon himself as a man, would not tamely submit to an unmerited insult from anyone. An instance of the difference I was some years ago a witness to. The son of an eminent grazier in Munster, with whom I was very intimately acquainted, was put apprentice to a linen draper in the north. In company with some others, riding through a fair, where he happened to find the people very much crowded, and of course his progress impeded, he forgot himself, and imagining that he was in a fair in his own country, and wishing to get forward, he lifted up his whip in a threatening manner to clear the rabble out of his way but he did not actually strike anyone. Upon this, a number of them, not less than twenty turned on him; one seized his bridle; others lifted their sticks, when a gentleman of the company, well known to many of them, rode forward and said that the young man had dined with him, and had taken too much claret; at which this man called out immediately to the rest, 'Let the poor boy pass on quietly: he's drunk.' If it had not been for the stratagem of this gentleman, I know not what might have been the consequence.

John Gough also remarked on the unpopularity of the tithe proctors. The tithes were a tax levied for the support of the established church on those who occupied agricultural land. Needless to say, the people had enough to do to cope with the demands of their landlords and to contribute towards the support of their own priests: the demands of the tithe proctors in support of what the vast majority of the people regarded as a heretical church was the last straw. Gough quoted from a survey made in county Offaly in his time:

THE DEMANDS for tithe vary at the will of the proctor or incumbent; rich farmers who have much corn seldom pay any for potatoes. This tax falls chiefly on the poor cotters, who pay by the perch, sometimes the full value. In some parts, those poor people suffer their tithe to be drawn, rather than pay the demand, which is often above the value. Tithes are not often in kind; but the proctors sometimes delay their valuation, which obliges the farmers to keep their corn on the ground to its great injury; this has often been complained of; and repeated notices given to the proctors in vain.

Though the clergy in general are reasonable in their demands, yet when tithes are let, or left to proctors, many complaints must arise. The poor man

An evicted family, c. 1840

will pay the proctor his demand, rather than be cited to the bishop's court, or than keep his corn on the ground, when the grazing of his stables is necessary to him; many instances hereof might be stated. In this county tithes are a greater cause of complaint than in others, as it is almost the only part of Leinster in which tithe is demanded for potatoes, which seems un-reasonable, as few counties have more corn. Hence tithes, whether they are a real grievance or not, have always been the pretence for disturbance; hence the prevalence of *Whiteboys*, some years ago; hence, the farmers seem to consider themselves scarcely affected by any other grievance, it is the first object in their minds; and more so here than in many other places, as the inhabitants and rich farmers are almost all Roman Catholics, who think it hard to support two establishments, and pay so much for a worship from which they receive no benefit.

The tithes are usually valued by proctors after harvest; sometimes he meets the farmers at public houses (another source of evil) to settle with them. Sometimes the incumbent agrees himself; the farmer then quits his work, to go to him repeatedly, whose time is taken up in making bargains. The tithes are paid half yearly, in November and May.

All the evils produced by the present mode of paying the clergy, are too numerous to enlarge upon.

It was not until the early 1830s that an organised resistance to the payment of tithes began. Frequent battles took place in which the proctors called in the aid of the military and the police and the government, alarmed at the strength of the opposition, passed a drastic coercion act to deal with the situation in 1833. That same year the Church Temporalities Act was passed, which reduced the number of Protestant bishops and abolished a rate levied for the maintenance of Protestant churches; and five years later the Tithe Bill of 1838 reduced the tithes by twenty-five per cent and converted them into a charge on the land, payable by the landlord.

As the years went by, the condition of the labourers deteriorated. A few years before the great famine, Mr and Mrs Hall witnessed evictions in the midlands. Their interest in the plight of the cottiers was first aroused by a newspaper's account of a case brought before the quarter sessions court at Trim. They copied the following account, they assure us, without the change of a sentence:

ON THE CONCLUSION of the registry, and commencement of the Crown business, Mr Despard, R.M., said that, by direction of the petty sessions bench of Athboy, he was desired to bring a case of nuisance under the consideration of the court of quarter sessions, in order to obtain an order to have the nuisance abated by the police. The case was a simple one: an individual had built a house within thirty feet of the centre of the road, at Moyagher, in this county, and the law made such an erection a nuisance. The party had been fined ten pounds by the magistrates at petty sessions, but had no goods out of which the amount could be levied, and the only way in which the nuisance could be got rid of was by order from the quarter sessions bench to the police. The court had jurisdiction under the Grand Jury Act. Mr Hinds, one of the practitioners of the court, desired to know was the erection he alluded to built in what was known as the church-yard, and was the application for the purpose of removing one of those unfortunate wretches who, guilty of no crime, were turned adrift on the world, under the present clearing out system, and who might have taken up his abode among the graves in the churchyard? Captain Despard said he was prepared to prove the case he had laid before the bench, and proceeded to examine Chief Constable of Police Greaves, who said he has measured from the centre of the road to the erection, and there were not thirty feet to the wood supporting the entrance; it came within thirty feet by two or three inches. Mr Ford desired to know from Mr Greaves, was not what he was describing as a building, within thirty feet of the centre of the road, a hole dug through the road ditch into the churchyard, in which the poor man and his family lived? and was not what he described as a door, a piece of torn sack, hanging down in front of the hole? Mr Greaves replied, that he, Mr Ford, if he pleased, might call it a hole in the ditch. Mr Ford then stated he was agent to the gentleman who held the land of Moyagher from the provost, and begged to be permitted to interfere in this matter, lest it might be thought for a moment, that either he or his principal had any connexion whatsoever with the present proceeding. He himself had passed the place about three weeks ago, and what was termed an erection was literally what he described; it was a hole dug through the ditch into the churchyard, and in that wretched place was this very miserable habitation for a fellow-creature. The act referred to by Captain Despard, was the Grand Jury Act; now, that was a very recent statute, and Mr Ford submitted, that it should appear to the court that the erection complained of was made since the passing of the act. The Hon. Mr Plunket, the assistant barrister, after reading the section, agreed with Mr Ford, and thereupon Mr Despard directed the crier call Michael Brady—

he was the man himself; he might not have done so, but he thought, although the act did not direct it, yet that notice would be given to him, and he had, accordingly, caused notice to be served on him; and thereupon, Michael Brady, who appeared to be an able-bodied man, about forty-five years of age, came on the table. He was asked, when did he build the cabin in the churchyard? 'It is no cabin at all, your worships—it is only a hole in the churchyard,' was the reply. 'I'll tell your honours all about it: on the eighth of May last, I was turned out of my cabin by a decree. I was an under tenant only, and myself, and my wife, and my five children, were left without a house over our heads, and I could not get a house from any one—because it is now very hard for a poor man to get a house from any one, for the people won't let them in for fear of displeasing the gentlemen, and so I could not get

A 'scalp', an evicted man's shelter, near Kilrush, 1843

a house, and no one would let me in; and, after lying nine nights out in the ditches, I did not know what to do, as no one dared take pity on me; and as the children would be perished if they slept out any longer, I dug in the churchyard, seeing that another person like me had gone to live there before me; and we had lived there ever since, and I do not know where to go if your honours turn me out of that.' The order of the court was that the nuisance should be abated by the police; but the order not to issue until the workhouse of Kells union, in which district the place is situate, shall be opened.

The cabins of the small farmers differed little from those of the agricultural labourers in the depressed areas of the southwest and west. Gustave de Beaumont, a Frenchman who visited Ireland in the thirties described a cabin built in a depressed area.

IMAGINE FOUR walls of dried mud, (which the rain, as it falls, easily restores to its primitive condition) having for its roof a little straw or some sods, for its chimney a hole cut in the roof, or very frequently the door through which alone the smoke finds an issue. One single apartment contains father, mother, children and sometimes a grandfather or a grandmother; there is no furniture in the wretched hovel; a single bed of straw serves the entire family. Five or six half-naked children may be seen crouched near a miserable fire, the ashes of which cover a few potatoes, the sole nourishment of the family. In the midst of all lies a dirty pig, the only thriving inhabitant of the place, for he lives in filth. The presence of the pig in an Irish hovel may at first seem an indication of misery; on the contrary, it is a sign of comparative comfort. Indigence is still more extreme in the hovel where no pig is to be found . . . I have just described the dwelling of the Irish farmer or agricultural labourer.

Almost half the population in 1841 lived in one roomed houses about eighteen feet long and twelve feet wide. Where overcrowding was a problem the danger of typhus increased, and fever often raged on the islands from Tory to Cape Clear. Johann Georg Köhl, sometime city librarian at Bremen, who came to Ireland in 1842, wrote:

48

THE INHABITANTS of the little Irish island of Cape Clear suffered so much from a scarcity of fuel in 1839, that they came together and cast lots, which first, and which second and third, should tear down his cabin in order to warm the dwellings of the others with its materials. But the fever-plague was only increased by this proceeding; for as they were all crowded together in narrow rooms, and admitted no fresh air into their houses, the infection spread with still greater violence. Besides, in wet and cold years the poor are often compelled to mend the roofs of their houses with the straw which they had destined for their beds; and on these occasions, instead of fresh straw, they have to sleep upon old, or most probably upon none at all. All the misery that a wet year thus produces in Ireland (and on account of the peculiar nature of the country, it produces more than with us) tends to increase typhus, and to fill the fever hospitals. Whilst other lands always wish for rain, Ireland generally longs for dry weather: the ground retains so much moisture that a dry year is never injurious. The potatoes then turn out best, and the turf is most easily made; and turf and potatoes are here the foundation of all earthly happiness, and even of existence itself, the true *nervus omnium rerum* as money is in other lands.

What might have happened had the landlords of Ireland been conscientious, or as the case may be, financially capable of bettering the lot of their tenants, may be guessed at by reading any of the glowing accounts written by pre-famine travellers in the baronies of Forth and Bargy in south-east Wexford. Here the gentry were of the people; landlord and tenant were descended from the Norman and Flemish settlers of the twelfth and thirteenth centuries. The social gap between the two classes was as wide as it was in every other part of Ireland but a mutual respect had existed here for centuries. (Even the British government recognised this fact: after the rebellion of 1798, it decided in the interests of peace not to confiscate the demesnes of the landlords Harvey and Colclough, who had led their tenantry into battle.) The Halls knew Wexford intimately, and in 1842 they wrote that its prosperity

IS APPARENT not only in its external aspect—the skilfully farmed fields, the comfortable cottages, the barns

49

A game of cards, from a painting by Erskine Nicol

attached to every farmyard, the well trimmed hedgerows, the neat gardens stocked with other vegetables than potatoes, and the acre of beans—the peasantry are better fed than we have seen them in any other part of Ireland, and have an air of sturdy independence. They very rarely owe any debt to their landlords except 'goodwill', and an arrear of rent is a thing seldom heard of. A peasant is never seen without shoes and stockings, and a young woman very rarely without a bonnet. Those who encounter an illdressed or dirty person along the roads may be very sure they have met a stranger. The interior of their cottages is in corresponding order. The most fastidious guest may not hesitate to dine under the thatched roof of a labourer of the southern baronies. They are a proud people—proud of their ancient names, and their advanced civilisation. Of native beggars there are none in the district. Such as have no personal means of support apply to their more fortunate neighbours and neither consider themselves, nor are they considered by others, as beggars.

50

In every farmhouse a sack of meal was formerly placed open in the kitchen, with a plate, to be dealt out in charity to the wandering poor; whilst food and lodging was to be found wherever it was required.

Johnstown Castle was the seat of one of the principal landlords in the southern baronies, and a model landlord he was. The Halls continued:

TO EXHIBIT what may be done in Ireland, I refer to this estate, unencumbered, yielding to its possessor an immense annual income, spent by himself in the country, the money as it were returned to the tenant, with the rich interest of protection and kindness. Three hundred labourers constantly employed on this estate; a school-house, beautiful to look at, and useful in its construction, built and supported without regard to expense, at the gate leading to the princely demesne; the master, a man qualified in every respect of his occupation; no religious distinction made, and none thought of, either by the learned or the learner. Cottages built in the midst of flourishing gardens; roses and woodbines clustering round their windows; and landlord doubling the amount of whatever prizes his tenants may receive from agricultural societies, as encouragements to good conduct. No wild pigs, no beggars, no dunghills, no fear, few whiskey-shops, little quarrelling, very little idleness; clean, healthy, well-dressed children, the prettiest girls and 'neatest boys' in Ireland. You ask of the landlord's and landlady's religion: both are members of the Church of England; some of their servants are Catholics, some Protestants. I never heard the sound of religious difference in their household. By night and by day their house is open to relieve either sorrow or sickness; there are no traces of extravagance in their arrangements, though the park is full of deer, and the merry horn frequently calls forth the stag-hounds to the chase. This is not an Irish Utopia of my own creation; any one sceptical as to the possibility of Irish civilisation may go to Wexford . . .

The tenant farmers were quite well off, according to the Halls, 'wherever the landlord pursued the policy of live and let live'. In county Down, for instance, they encountered

51

ONLY ADMIRABLY constructed farm-houses, well-furnished with barns and byres, cornfields and pasture lands, the natural richness of which had been enhanced by industry and well-applied science; every dwelling bore numerous tokens of comfort; every peasant looked cheerful and happy.

More than one tourist came to the conclusion that in places where the estate was unencumbered and its owner prepared to live at home rather than in England, the tenant farmer's standard of living was often higher than in the neighbouring island. The Halls complimented the Irish farmers on their custom of neighbourly co-operation on the land, called in Irish, *an meitheal*. It showed, they said, what the Irish farmer could do 'if only he were given a chance'.

The following passage refers to Island Magee in Antrim, but the custom was common all over the country:

FROM THE largest to the smallest farmer, this habit is, more or less, observed, and to such an extent that at harvest, or at other seasons of brisk labour, very few hired, daily-paid labourers are employed in the place. The servants (hired by the half-year) of one farmer, together with the family, work on the farm of another person, on the occasions of ploughing, setting potatoes, and at harvest in conjunction with the master, family, family and servants of the other farm, who in return co-operate with horse labour, and in every labour. It would appear that the small holders who have not horses are the most benefited by this custom. It may be inconvenient to them to pay for ploughing their farms; they therefore have them ploughed by a neighbour, to whom in return they yield labour, most frequently at the time of harvest, in this proportion, viz., for a day's ploughing with two horses they give eight days work of man or woman. This principle of neighbouring has been found from long observance most beneficial, and has a great tendency to maintain good and kindly feeling in a country community.

Every traveller in pre-famine Ireland found the country people of all classes a gay hospitable people. Sir John Carr, a Devonshire landowner, who toured Ireland in 1806, wrote:

> THEIR HOSPITALITY when their circumstances are not too wretched to display it, is remarkably great. The neighbour or the stranger finds every man's door open, and to walk in without ceremony at mealtime, and to partake of his bowl of potatoes, is always sure to give pleasure to every one of the house, and the pig is turned out to make room for the gentleman. If the visitor can relate a lively tale, or play upon any instrument, all the family is in smiles, and the young will begin a merry dance, whilst the old will smoke after one another out of the same pipe, and entertain each other with stories. A gentleman of an erratic turn was pointed out to me, who with his flute in his hand, a clean pair of stockings and a shirt in his pocket, wandered through the country every summer; wherever he stopped the face of a stranger made him welcome, and the sight of his instrument doubly so; the best seat, if they had any, the best potatoes and new milk, were allotted for his dinner; and clean straw, and sometimes a pair of sheets formed his bed; which, although frequently not a bed of roses, was always rendered welcome by fatigue, and the peculiar bias of his mind.

The hospitality of the people was also attested to by Mrs Asenath Nicholson of New York, who came to Ireland in 1844. In her book, *Ireland's Welcome to the Stranger,* the kindly evangelist told of a visit to the house of a Kilkenny girl she had once employed in America.

> THE WHOLE parish was now in a stir, work was suspended, and a general levee held. They talked of building bonfires; they talked of uniting and buying a sheep to kill, though not one had eaten a dinner of flesh since Christmas. The grey-headed and the little child were there to welcome me, to thank me for 'thinking of the like of such poor bodies', and from some miles around visitors called before the setting of the sun to look at the American stranger, and bid her God-speed. 'What will she ate, the cratur? It's not the potato that raired her.' Two

53

children begged the honour of going seven miles in quest of fruit, and went. Night and rain overtook them, yet they persevered, slept away through the night, and cheerfully returned the next day with two pears and a spoonful of blackberries, which was all they could procure. All went away sorrowful that so 'nice a body should be so trated', and all asked me to visit their cabins, 'though they were not fittin' for such a lady'.

The next morning Anne again called to say she had been sent to invite me to attend a field dance which was to be on the next day, the Sabbath. In surprise I was about to answer, when Anne said, 'I knew you would not, and told them so, but they begged I would say that they had no other day, as all were at work, and sure God wouldn't be hard upon 'em, when they had no other time, and could do nothing else for the stranger.' I thanked them heartily for their kind feelings, and declined. Judge my confusion, when about sunset on Sabbath evening, just after returning from Johnstown, where I had attended church, the cabin door opened, and a crowd of all ages walked in, decently attired for the day, and without the usual welcomes or any apology, the hero who first introduced me seated himself at my side, took out his flute, wet his fingers, saying, 'This is for you, Mrs N., and what will you have?' A company was arranged for the dance, and so confounded was I that I only murmured, 'I cannot tell.' He struck up an Irish air, and the dance began. I had nothing to say, taken by surprise as I was; my only strength was to sit still.

This dance finished, the eldest son of my hostess advanced, made a low bow, and invited me to lead the next dance. I looked on his glossy black slippers, his blue stockings snugly fitted up to the knee, his corduroys above them, his blue coat and brass buttons, and had no reason to hope that, at my age of nearly half a century, I could ever expect another like offer. However, I was not urged to accept it. Improper as it might appear, it was done as a civility, which, as a guest in his mother's house and a stranger, he thought, and all thought (as I was afterwards told) he owed me. The cabin was too small to contain the three score and ten who had assembled, and with one simultaneous movement, without speaking, all rushed out, bearing me along, and placed me upon a cart before the door, the player at my right hand. And then an amazing dance began. Not a laugh—not a loud word was heard; but as soberly as though they were in a funeral procession, they danced for an hour, wholly for my amusement, and for my welcome. Then each approached, gave me the hand, bade me God-speed, leaped over the stile, and in stillness walked away. It was a true and hearty Irish welcome, in which the aged as well as the young participated.

Mrs Nicholson, like many another traveller, found that the most striking paradox of the Irish scene was that even that section of the community who lived in wretched conditions looked very healthy and well-fed. Many travellers underestimated the nutritional value of a staple fare of potatoes washed down by milk or buttermilk, and confessed failure to account for the vitality of the people. Sir John Carr found that in a mountain district in Wicklow in 1806—

UPON AN average, a man, his wife, and four children, will eat thirty-seven pounds of potatoes a day. The family live upon potatoes and buttermilk six days a week; the Sabbath is generally celebrated by bacon and greens. A whimsical anecdote is related of an Irish potato. An Englishman, seeing a number of fine florid children in a cabin, said to the father: 'How do your countrymen contrive to have so many fine children?' 'By Jasus, it is the potato, sir,' said he.

FACTION FIGHTS, WEDDINGS AND WAKES

T HE GREAT weakness of the Irish, according to all the travellers, was
their fondness of fighting and drinking. Farmers and labourers alike
managed to combine the two at fairs and patrons and more than one traveller
expressed his horror at the goings on in country districts on saints' feast days.

In 1818 the Catholic bishop of Cork forbade his flock to attend the patron
at Gougane because he felt that 'the patron was selected for the purpose of
contest by hostile factions'. Henry Inglis, the Scots journalist, was one of the
many travellers who witnessed the faction fights of rural Ireland. The one
Inglis described took place in Connemara, at the close of a patron:

ALL WAS QUIET when I reached the
ground; and I was warmly welcomed as a stranger by many who invited me
into their tents. Of course I accepted the invitation; and the pure potheen
circulated freely.

By and by, however, some boastful expression of a Joyce appeared to
give offence to several at the far end of the tent; and something loud and
contemptuous was spoken of by two or three in a breath. The language
which, in compliment to me, had been English, suddenly changed to Irish.
Two or three glasses of potheen were quickly gulped by most of the boys;
and the innkeeper who had accompanied me, and who sat by me, whispered
that there would soon be some fighting. I had seen abundance of fighting on a
small scale, in Ireland; but I confess, I had been barbarous enough to wish I
might see a regular faction fight: and now I was likely to be gratified. Taking

Right
A faction fighter, from a painting by
Erskine Nicol

Below
A faction fight

the hint of the innkeeper, I shook hands with the 'boys' nearest to me, right and left; and taking advantage of a sudden burst of voices, I stepped over my bench and, retiring from my tent, took up a safe position on some neighbouring rocks.

I had not long to wait: out sallied the Joyces and a score of other 'boys' from several tents at once, as if there had been some preconcerted signal; and the flourishing of shillelaghs did not long precede the using of them. Any one to see an Irish fight for the first time would conclude that a score or two must inevitably be put *hors de combat*. The very flourish of a regular shillelagh, and the shout that accompanies it, seem to be the immediate precursors of a fractured skull; but the affair, though bad enough, is not so fatal as it appears to be: the shillelaghs, no doubt, do sometimes descend upon a head, which is forthwith a broken head; but they oftener descend upon each other: and the fight soon becomes one of personal strength. The parties close and grapple; and the most powerful man throws his adversary: fair play is but little attended to: two or three often attack a single man; nor is there a cessation of blows, even when a man is on the ground. On the present occasion, five or six were disabled: but there was no homicide; and after a scrimmage, which lasted perhaps ten minutes, the Joyces remained masters of the field. The women took no part in the fight; but they are not always so backward: it is chiefly, however, when stones are the weapons, that women take a part, by supplying the combatants with missiles. When the fight ended, there were not many remaining, excepting those who were still in the tents, and who chanced to be of neither faction. Most of the women had left the place when the quarrel began, and some of the men too. I noticed, after the fight, that some, who had been opposed to each other, shook hands and kissed; and appeared as good friends as before.

The funeral customs of rural Ireland amazed the travellers. Miss Plumptre devoted a few pages of her 1814 *Narrative* to them but it is obvious that she had not actually been present at a wake—she thought that the *mná caointe* (keening women) were men. This is part of Mr and Mrs Hall's account of a Munster wake:

THE FORMALITIES commence almost

immediately after life has ceased. The corpse is at once laid out, and the wake begins, the priest having been first summoned to say mass for the repose of the departed soul, which he generally does in the apartment in which the body reposes! It is regarded by the friends of the deceased as a sacred duty to watch by the corpse until laid in the grave; and only less sacred is the duty of attending it thither.

The ceremonies differ somewhat in various districts, but only in a few minor and unimportant particulars. The body, decently laid out on a table or bed, is covered with white linen, and not unfrequently adorned with black ribbons, if an adult; white, if the party be unmarried; and flowers, if a child. Close by it, or upon it, are plates of tobacco and snuff; around it are lighted candles. Usually a quantity of salt is laid upon it also. The women of the household range themselves at either side, and the keen (*caoine*) at once

Keening women at a wake, c. 1843

commences. They rise with one accord and, moving their bodies with a slow motion to and fro, their arms apart, they continue to keep up a heart-rending cry. This cry is interrupted for a while to give the *ban caointhe* (the leading keener), an opportunity of commencing. At the close of every stanza of the dirge, the cry is repeated, to fill up, as it were, the pause, and then dropped; the woman then again proceeds with the dirge, and so on to the close. The only interruption which this manner of conducting a wake suffers is from the entrance of some relative of the deceased, who, living remote, or from some other cause, may not have been in at the commencement. In this case, the *ban caointhe* ceases, all the women rise and begin the cry, which is continued until the newcomer has cried enough. During the pauses of the women's wailing, the men, seated in groups by the fire, or in the corners of the room, are indulging in jokes, exchanging repartees, and bantering each other, some about their sweethearts, and some about their wives, or talking over the affairs of the day—prices and politics, priests and parsons, the all-engrossing subjects of Irish conversation.

The keener is usually paid for her services—the charge varying from a crown to a pound, according to the circumstances of the employer. They

> live upon the dead,
> By letting out their persons by the hour
> To mimic sorrow when the heart's not sad.

It often happens, however, that the family has some friend or relation, rich in the gift of poetry; and who will for love of her kin give the unbought eulogy to the memory of the deceased. The Irish language, bold, forcible, and comprehensive, full of the most striking epithets and idiomatic beauties, is peculiarly adapted for either praise or satire—its blessings are singularly touching and expressive, and its curses wonderfully strong, bitter and biting. The rapidity and ease with which both are uttered, and the epigrammatic force of each concluding stanza of the keen, generally bring tears to the eyes of the most indifferent spectator, or produce a state of terrible excitement. The dramatic effect of the scene is very powerful: the darkness of the death-chamber, illumined only by candles that glare upon the corpse, the manner of repetition or acknowledgement that runs round when the keener gives out a sentence, the deep, yet suppressed sobs of the nearer relatives, and the stormy, uncontrollable cry of the widow or bereaved husband when allusion is made

60

to the domestic virtues of the deceased—all heighten the effect of the keen; but in the open air, winding round some mountain pass, when a priest, or person greatly beloved and respected, is carried to the grave, and the keen, swelled by a thousand voices, is borne upon the mountain echoes—it is then absolutely magnificent.

The keener having finished a stanza of the keen, sets up the wail in which all the mourners join. Then a momentary silence ensues, when the keener commences again, and so on—each stanza ending in the wail. The keen usually consists in an address to the corpse, asking him why did he die? etc., or a description of his person, qualifications, riches, etc.; it is altogether extemporaneous; and it is sometimes astonishing to observe with what facility the keener will put the verses together, and shape her poetical images to the case of the person before her. This, of course, can only appear strongly to a person acquainted with the language, as any merit which these compositions possess is much obscured in a translation.

The keener is almost invariably an aged woman; or if she be comparatively young, the habits of her life make her look old. We remember one; we can never forget a scene in which she played a conspicuous part. A young man had been shot by the police as he was resisting a warrant for his arrest. He was of 'decent people', and had a 'fine wake'. The woman, when we entered the apartment, was sitting on a low stool by the side of the corpse. Her long black uncombed locks were hanging about her shoulders; her eyes were the deep set grey peculiar to the country, and which are capable of every expression, from the bitterest hatred and the direst revenge to the softest and warmest affection. Her large blue cloak was confined at her throat; but not so closely as to conceal the outline of her figure, thin and gaunt, but exceedingly lithesome. When she arose, as if by sudden inspiration, first holding out her hands over the body, and then tossing them wildly above her head, she continued her chant in a low monotonous tone, occasionally breaking into a style earnest and animated; and using every variety of attitude to give emphasis to her words, and enforce her description of the virtues and good qualities of the deceased. 'Swift and sure was his foot', she said, 'on hill and valley. His shadow struck terror to his foes; he could look the sun in the face like an eagle; the whirl of his weapon through the air was fast and terrible as the lightning. There had been full and plenty in his father's house, and the traveller never left it empty; but the tyrants had taken all except his heart's blood—and that they took at last. The girls of the mountain may cry by the running streams, and weep for the flower of the country—but he would return no more. He was the last of his father's house; but his people were many both on hill and valley; and they would revenge his death!' Then, kneeling, she clenched her hands together, and cursed bitter curses against whoever had aimed the fatal bullet—curses which illustrate but too forcibly the fervour of Irish hatred. 'May the light fade from your eyes, so that you may never see what you love! May the grass grow at your door! May you fade into nothing like snow in summer! May your own blood rise against ye, and the sweetest drink ye take be the bittherest cup of sorrow! May ye die without benefit of priest or clergy!' To each curse there was a deep 'Amen', which the *ban caointhe* paused to hear, then resumed her maledictions.

Thomas Crofton Croker was a Corkman who used his leisure chiefly in the study of the people of the south of Ireland. In 1824 he published *Researches in the South of Ireland,* and in a chapter dealing with funeral customs he mentioned the people's fear of the banshee.

                    A CURIOUS spirit, and one I believe peculiar to Ireland, is the banshee . . . a small, shrivelled old woman with long white hair, supposed to be peculiarly attached to old houses or families, and to announce the approaching dissolution of any members by mournful lamentations. This fairy attendant is considered as highly honourable.

According to Mr and Mrs Hall, who seemed to believe in her, the following is a correct notation of the wail of the Banshee:

Both Mrs Plumptre and Mrs Hall assure us that weddings in rural Ireland were conducted with commendable decorum. The poteen may have flowed freely but fighting didn't break out as often as the travellers expected it would. Here is the Halls' description of an Irish country wedding:

OUR READERS will bear in mind that we are describing a picture as exhibited in the cottage of a small farmer, where there is comparative abundance; and on such occasions the national hospitality is never bounded by prudence: far less merry, and infinitely less plentiful of good cheer, is the scene enacted within one of the common cabins of the hard-handed labourer, where, not unfrequently, the marriage feast is little more than a dish of potatoes and a jug of sweet milk.

If the bride's father or brother be a strong farmer, who can afford to furnish a good dinner, the marriage takes place at the bride's house, the bridegroom bringing with him as many of his friends as choose to accompany him. It is not uncommon for the priest's collection to amount to twenty, thirty and sometimes forty or fifty pounds where the parties are comfortable. The time most in favour for celebrating weddings is just before Lent. The guests are always numerous, and consist of all ranks, from the lord and lady of the manor, squireens, farmers, down to the common labourer—wives, of course, included. Perfect equality prevails on this occasion, and yet the natural courtesy of the Irish character prevents any disturbance of social order—everyone keeps his place, while, at the same time, the utmost freedom reigns.

The priest sits at the head of the table, near him the bride and bridegroom, the helpers of the clergyman, and the more respectable guests; the other guests occupy the remainder of the table, which extends the whole length of the barn—in which the dinner generally takes place. Immediately the cloth is removed, the priest marries the young couple, and then the bride cake is brought in and placed before the priest, who, putting on his stole, blesses it, and cuts it up into small slices which are handed round in a large dish among the guests. Each guest takes a slice of the cake, and lays down in place of it a donation for the priest, consisting of pounds, crowns, or shillings, according to the ability of the donor. After that, wine and punch go round. In the course of an hour or so, part of the range of tables is removed and the musicians—usually a piper and a fiddler, strike up.

An Irish dancer

First single parties dance reels, jigs and doubles. The last is a species of dance very difficult to describe—it is, however, the male partner who 'shows off', and the best idea we can give of it is that it consists in striking the ground very rapidly with the heel and toe, or with the toes of each foot alternately. The perfection of this motion consists, besides its rapidity, in the fury in which it is performed. A stranger, not hearing the music, and seeing only the dancer, would be sure to imagine he was killing a rat; nor would it be very safe to have this dance performed by a stout fellow in a frail loft. Country dances

64

now succeed, in which, as in the single dances, priest and laic, old and young, rich and poor, the master and his maid, the landlord and the tenant's daughter, all join together without distinction. Yet it is pleasing to observe how the peasants return on such occasions the condescension of their superiors with additional respect.

During the intervals of the dance drinking is resumed; and though on these occasions it was often carried to excess we never knew, nor ever met, anyone who knew of anything like a quarrel taking place at a country wedding. Indeed, we have seen people who were, as the saying goes, wicked in their liquor, get intoxicated at these joyous festivals, without manifesting ill temper—on the contrary, they have been remarkably entertaining, as if the general harmony had expelled the demon of discord. Songs are also sung in both Irish and English. In the course of the night a collection is made for the music and another for the poor. The dancing generally continues until morning, when the first intimation of breaking up is the dancing of a figure called Sir Roger de Coverley. As soon as that dance is over, all the more timid part of the female guests slip out of the barn to avoid the finale, which is as follows: The music striking up the quadrille air called *Voulez Vous Danser*, a gentleman goes round with a handkerchief which he throws round the neck of any lady he chooses, falls on his knees, gently pulls her down and kisses her; then giving her the handkerchief, continues a kind of trot round the barn; the lady does the same with any gentleman she likes, and giving him the handkerchief, catches the first gentleman by the skirts of his coat and trots after him round the barn. This is done alternately by all present, until all the young men and women are trotting round catching each other. They then form a ring round the last person who has the handkerchief, who selects a lady or gentleman, as the case may be, and after another kiss leads his or her partner to a seat. This is done until the whole circle is broken up; and thus terminates an Irish country wedding.

With regard to marriage, the Halls also mentioned that in Ireland, as in England, Shrove Tuesday night was 'pancake night', and that the old custom of pancake tossing then prevailed in every district in the south. The family group gathered around the fireside and each in turn tried his or her skill in tossing the cake.

Pancake night, drawn by Daniel Maclise

THE TOSSING of the first is always allotted to the eldest unmarried daughter of the host, who performs the task not altogether without trepidation, for much of her 'luck' during the year is supposed to depend upon her good or ill success on the occasion. She tosses it, and usually so cleverly as to receive it back again, without a ruffle on its surface, on its reverse, in the pan. Congratulations upon her fortune go round, and another makes the effort: perhaps this is a sad mischance; the pancake is either not turned or falls among the turf ashes; the unhappy

66

maiden is then doomed—she can have no chance of marrying for a year at least—while the girl who has been lucky is destined to have her 'pick of the boys' as soon as she likes. The cake she has tossed, she is at once called upon to share, and cutting it into as many slices as there are guests, she hands one to each: sometimes the mother's wedding-ring has been slipped into the batter out of which this first cake is made, and the person who receives the slice in which it is contained, is not only to be first married, but is to be doubly lucky in the matter of husband or wife. Men also are permitted, as in the instance pictured by Maclise, to have a chance; and it is a great source of amusement to jog their elbows at the important moment, and so compel them to 'toss the cake crooked'.

May Eve, the last day of April, was called Nettlemas night in Cork. The Halls tell us that on this night it was the custom for boys and girls to parade the streets with large bunches of nettles, 'availing themselves of the privilege to sting their lovers'. But by far the strangest custom relating to love and marriage they had ever heard of was commonplace on Achill Island.

A FEW DAYS before our arrival, an occurrence took place which we understood is by no means uncommon—a race for a wife. A young man, a carpenter, named Linchigan, applied to the father of a girl named Corrigan, for his daughter in marriage. A rival, called Lavelle, asked for her also, on the plea that as he was richer, 'he wouldn't ask so much with her'. Whereupon, the factions 'of the swains' were about to join issue and fight; when a peacemaker suggested that 'the boys should run for her'. The race was run accordingly, a distance of some miles up and down a mountain; Linchigan won, and wedded the maiden.

It is surprising how many of the customs mentioned by the travellers have survived to this day. The wren boys are a common sight in the southern towns and countryside still, as they go out on St Stephen's day performing their old mummeries more for sport than for financial gain. The Halls saw the wren boys in action in Cork.

The wren boys, c. 1843, drawn by Daniel Maclise

FOR SOME weeks preceding Christmas, crowds of village boys may be seen peering into the hedges, in search of the 'tiny wren'; and when one is discovered, the whole assemble and give eager chase to, until they have slain, the little bird. In the hunt, the utmost excitement prevails; shouting, screeching, and rushing; all sorts of missiles are flung at the puny mark; and, not infrequently, they light upon the head of some less innocent being. From bush to bush, from hedge to hedge, is the wren pursued until bagged with as much pride and pleasure as the cock of the woods by the more ambitious sportsman. The stranger is utterly at a loss to conceive the cause of this hubbub, or the motive for so much energy in pursuit of 'such small gear'. On the anniversary of St Stephen (26 December) the enigma is explained. Attached to a huge holly-bush, elevated on a pole, the bodies of several little wrens are borne about. This bush is an object of admiration in proportion to the number of dependent birds, and is carried through the streets in procession, by a troop of boys, among whom may be usually found 'children of a larger growth', shouting and roaring as they proceed along, and every now and then stopping before some popular house and there singing 'the wren boys' song.

To the words we have listened a score of times, and although we have found them often varied according to the wit or poetical capabilities of a leader of the party, and have frequently heard them drawled out to an apparently interminable length, the following specimen will probably satisfy our readers as to the merit of the composition:

> The wran, the wran, the king of all birds,
> St Stephen's day was cot in the furze,
> Although he is little his family's grate,
> Put yer hand in yer pocket and give us a trate.
>   Sing holly, sing ivy—sing ivy, sing holly,
>   A drop just to drink it would drown melancholy.
> And if you dhraw it ov the best,
> I hope in heaven yer sowl will rest,
> But if you dhraw it ov the small
> It won't agree wid de wran boys at all.

Of course contributions are levied in many quarters, and the evening is, or rather was, occupied in drinking out the sum total of the day's collection.

Among the young men in the country areas, hurling was a favourite sport. The Halls were particularly impressed by the skill and excitement of a game they saw played between two parishes in Kerry.

IT IS A FINE, manly exercise, with sufficient of danger to produce excitement; and is, indeed, par excellence, *the* game of the peasantry of Ireland. To be an expert hurler, a man must possess athletic powers of no ordinary character; he must have a quick eye, a ready hand, and a strong arm; he must be a good runner, a skilful wrestler, and withal patient as well as resolute. In some respects, it resembles cricket; but the rules, and the form of the bats, are altogether different; the bat of the cricketer being straight and that of the hurler crooked.

The forms of the game are these: the players, sometimes to the number of fifty or sixty, being chosen for each side, they are arranged (usually barefoot) in two opposing ranks, with their hurleys crossed, to await the tossing up of the ball, the wickets or goals being previously fixed at the extremities of the hurling-green, which, from the nature of the play, is required to be a level extensive plain. Then, there are two picked men chosen to keep the goal on each side, over whom the opposing party places equally tried men as a counterpoise; the duty of these goal-keepers being to arrest the ball in case of its near approach to that station, and return it back towards that of the opposite party, while those placed over them exert all their energies to drive it through the wicket. All preliminaries being adjusted, the leaders take their places in the centre. A person is chosen to throw up the ball, which is done as straight as possible, when the whole party, withdrawing their hurleys, stand with them elevated, to receive and strike it in its descent; now comes the crash of mimic war, hurleys rattle against hurleys—the ball is struck and re-struck, often for several minutes, without advancing much nearer to either goal; and when someone is lucky enough to get a clear 'puck' at it, it is sent flying over the field. It is now followed by the entire party at their utmost speed; the men grapple, wrestle, and toss each other with amazing agility, neither victor nor vanquished waiting to take breath, but following the course of the rolling and flying prize; the best runners watch each other, and keep almost shoulder to shoulder through the play, and the best wrestlers keep as close on them as possible, to arrest or impede their progress. The ball must not be taken from the ground by the hand; and the tact and skill shown in taking it on the point of the hurley, and running with it half the length of the field, and when too closely pressed, striking it towards the goal, is a matter of astonishment to those who are but slightly acquainted with the play. At the goal is the chief brunt of the battle. The goal-keepers receive the prize, and are opposed by those set over them; the struggle is tremendous— every power of strength and skill is exerted; while the parties from opposite sides of the field run at full speed to support their men engaged in the conflict; then the tossing and straining is at its height; the men often lying in dozens side by side on the grass, while the ball is returned by some strong arm again, flying above their heads, towards the other goal. Thus, for hours has the contention been carried on, and frequently the darkness of night arrests the game without giving victory to either side.

Young hurlers taking a rest, c. 1843

Prince Pückler-Muskau spent a lot of his time among the landed classes—mainly among the strong farmers whose interests were similar to his own. He went to see them enjoying themselves at Galway races and he went hunting with them near Cashel. He was given a warm welcome in Tipperary, where it was known that he had been received by O'Connell, the 'man of the people'.

I WAS ON horseback by six o'clock, on my way to breakfast at Captain S———'s country-house, where the sportsmen were to rendezvous for a hare-hunt. I found six or seven sturdy squires assembled; they do not think much, but their life is all the more gay and careless. After we had eaten and drank the most heterogeneous things—coffee, tea, whiskey, wine, eggs, beef-steaks, honey, mutton kidneys, cakes, bread and butter, one after another—the company seated themselves on two large cars, and took the direction of the Galtee mountains; where, at a distance of about eight miles, the hounds and horses were waiting for us. The weather was fine, and the ride very pleasant, along a ridge of hills commanding a full view of the fruitful plain, enclosed by mountains and richly varied by a multitude of gentlemen's seats and ruins which are scattered over the whole level country. I enjoyed these beauties, as usual, alone; my companions had only dogs and horses in their heads.

On our arrival at the appointed place of meeting, the horses were there, but no dogs. There were, however, a great many gentlemen, and instead of hunting hares we now all traversed the fields in every direction in search of the stray hounds. The sort of riding on these occasions is a thing of which people in our country can form no idea. Although most of the fields are enclosed by stone hedges from three to six feet high, and either piled loosely together or regularly cemented, and some of them edged by ditches; or strong walls of earth and stones pointed at the top, from five to seven feet high, with a ditch on one, sometimes on both sides—all this is not admitted as any pretext whatever for the riders to deviate from a straight line. If I mistake not, I have already described to you how wonderfully the horses here leap; the sagacity is also admirable with which they distinguish a loose hedge from a firm one, one recently thrown up, from one hardened by time. The loose ones they spring over at one leap—'clear them', according to the technical expression; but they take the firm ones more easily, making a sort of halt at the top.

All this takes place equally well in a full gallop, or, with the utmost coolness, at a foot pace, or with a very short run. Some gentlemen fell, but were only laughed at; for a man who does not break his neck on the spot must look for no pity, but on the contrary, ridicule. Others dismounted at very bad places, and their docile steeds leaped without them, and then stood still, grazing while their riders climbed over. I can assure you I very often thought I should be compelled to follow their example, but Captain S———, who knew the excellent horse on which he had mounted me, and was always by my side, encouraged me to trust with perfect security to the admirable creature; so that at the end of the day I had acquired a very considerable reputation even among 'fox hunters'. Certainly it is only in Ireland one sees all that horses are capable of; the English are far behind them in this respect. Wherever a man could get through, my horse found means to do so in one way or other, leaping crawling, or scrambling. Even in swampy places where he sank up to his girths, he laboured through without the least hurry or agitation, where a more lively and timorous horse, though equally strong, would certainly never have made his way. Such a horse on a field of battle would be beyond all price; but only very early and perfect training, joined to the excellence of the breed, can produce such a one. Experience shows that a peculiar bent of education, continued through centuries, ends in rendering the superinduced qualities natural even in animals. I saw pointers in England which, without any training, stood still and pointed as decidedly the first time they were taken out shooting, as if they had been ever so carefully trained.

The price of these admirable horses was extremely reasonable ten years ago, but since the English have begun to buy them for hunting, it is greatly raised, and an Irish hunter of the quality of the one I rode today would fetch from a hundred and fifty to two hundred guineas. At the Galway races I saw a celebrated blood-hunter, for which Lord Cl——— had given the latter sum. He had won every steeplechase he had ever run; was as light as he was powerful, swift as the wind, a child could manage him, and no hedge was too high, no ditch too wide for him.

At length we found the dogs: the men who had the care of them having got completely drunk. Our hunt did not end till the approach of twilight. It was become excessively cold, and the flickering fire, with the table spread before it, shone most agreeably upon us on our arrival at Captain S———'s house. A genuine sportsman's and bachelor's feast followed. There was no

Galway. View of the Corrib from the Claddagh, 1840

attempt at show or elegance. Glasses, dishes, and all the furniture of the table, were of every variety of form and date: one man drank his wine out of a liqueur glass, another out of a champagne glass, the more thirsty out of tumblers. One ate with his great grand-father's knife and fork, his neighbour with a new green-handled one which the servant had just bought at Cashel fair. There were as many dogs as guests in the room: every man waited on himself; and the meats and potables were pushed on the table in abundance by an old woman and a heavy-fisted groom. The fare was by no means to be despised, nor the wine either, nor the poteen clandestinely distilled in the mountains, which I here tasted for the first time genuine and unadulterated. For sweetening a pudding, two large lumps of sugar were handed about, and we rubbed them together as the savages do sticks for kindling fire. That the drinking was on a vast and unlimited scale you may safely presume: but though many at last could not speak very articulately, yet no one attempted anything indecorous or ill-bred; and the few who were much excited enhanced the merriment by many a *bon mot* or droll story.

I am indebted for the great cordiality, I might say enthusiasm, with which I am received here, to my visit to the 'man of the people' with whom the curious believe me to be in God-knows-what connection. I am greeted with hurrahs in every village I ride through; and in Cashel, the market-place in which my inn stands, is daily filled with people who congregate at an early hour and cheer me every time I go out. Many press forward and ask leave to shake my hand, (a no very gentle operation), and are quite happy when they have accomplished this.

We rose from table very late. I was packed into my host's car with another gentleman, and set off for Cashel through an icy fog. Every individual ran out to my assistance. One would draw a pair of furred gloves on my hands; another lent me a cloak; a third tied a handkerchief round my neck; every man insisted on doing me some little service: and with many a 'God bless his Highness!' I was at length suffered to depart. The gentleman with me, Mr O'R——— was the most original, and the most drunk of any. Equally bent on doing me some kindness, he invariably made the matter worse than he found it. He unfastened my cloak, in trying to fasten it; tore off my handkerchief, instead of tying it; and fell upon me, in his efforts to make room. His poetical humour displayed itself as characteristically when we reached the Rock of Cashel. It was dreadfully cold, and the cloudless firmament twinkled and glittered as if bestrewn with diamonds. Between the road and the rock, however, a thick mist lay along the earth, and covered the whole surrounding country as with a veil, though it did not rise higher than to the foot of the ruin. Its base was invisible, and it appeared as if it stood built on a cloud in the blue aether, and in the midst of the stars. I had been admiring this striking nightscene some time, when my neighbour, whom I thought asleep, suddenly cried aloud, 'Ah, there is my glorious rock! look, how grand! and above all the sacred place where all my ancestors repose, and where I too shall lie in peace!' After a pause he tried in a fit of greater ecstacy to stand up, which but for me, would have ended in his falling from the carriage. As soon as he was firmly on his feet, he took off his hat reverently, and with a sort of devotion, at once affecting and burlesque, called out with tears in his eyes, 'God bless Almighty God! Glory to Him!' Notwithstanding the nonsense, I was touched by the feeling which broke through it, and in this, at least, I sympathised with all my soul.

The Prince enjoyed himself immensely at Galway races. Evidently steeple-chasing was a much more hazardous pursuit in the 1820s than it is nowadays. Here is part of Pückler-Muskau's description of the scene at Galway in 1828:

YOU MUST now accompany me to the 'racecourse', and see the running and leaping from the beginning . . . I confess that it far exceeded my expectations, and kept me in a state of intense anxiety; only one must leave pity and humanity at home, as you will see from what follows. The race-course is an elongated circle. On the left side is the starting post; opposite to it, on the right, is the goal. Between them, at the opposite points of the circumference, are built walls of stone without mortar, five feet high and two broad. The course, two English miles in length, is run over once and a half. You see then, from my description, that the first wall must be leaped twice, the second only once in each heat. Many horses run, but none is declared winner till he has beaten the others in two heats; so that this is often repeated three, four, or even five times, if a different horse comes in ahead each time. Today they ran four times; so that the winner, in a space of less than two hours, reckoning the intervals, ran twelve English miles at full speed and leaped the high wall twelve times! a fatigue which it is difficult to conceive how any horse can stand. Six gentlemen in elegant jockey dresses of coloured silk jackets and caps, leather breeches and top-boots, rode the 'race'. I had an excellent hunter belonging to the son of my host, and could therefore, by crossing the course, keep up perfectly well, and be present at every leap.

It is impossible not to have a favourite on such occasions. Mine, and indeed that of the public, was an extremely beautiful dark bay, called Game-cock, ridden by a gentleman in yellow, a handsome young man of good family, and a most admirable rider.

After him, the horse which pleased me the most was a dark brown mare called Rosina, ridden by a cousin of Captain B———; a bad rider, in sky blue. The third in goodness, in my opinion, Killarney, was a strong but not very handsome horse, ridden by a young man who showed more power of endurance than perfect horsemanship; his dress was crimson. The fourth gentleman, perhaps the most skilful, though not the strongest of the riders, rode a brown horse not remarkable in its appearance, and was dressed in brown. The other two deserve no mention, as they were *hors du jeu* from the beginning; they both fell at the first leap; the one sustained a severe injury on the head, the other came off with a slight concussion, but was disabled from riding again. Gamecock, who darted off with such fury that his rider could hardly hold him in, and flew, rather than leapt, over the walls, with incredible bounds, won the first heat with ease. Immediately after him came Rosina without her rider, whom she had thrown, and took the remaining of her leaps of her own accord with great grace. Gamecock was now so decidedly the favourite that the bets were five to one upon him: but the result was far different from these expectations, and very tragical. After this noble animal had distanced the other two in two successive heats, and had achieved the two first leaps in the most brilliant manner, he set his foot, in the third, on a loose stone which one of the less skilful horses had pushed down as he fell, and which it was not permitted to remove out of the course. He fell backward upon his rider with such violence that both lay motionless, when the other riders came up, took not the slightest notice of them, and accomplished the leap. After a few seconds Gamecock got up, but his rider did not recover his senses. A surgeon present soon pronounced his state to be hopeless; both his breast-bone and scull were fractured. His old father, who stood by when the accident happened, fell senseless on the ground, and his sister threw herself with heartrending cries on the yet palpitating though unconscious body. But the general sympathy was very slight. After the poor young man had been repeatedly bled, so that he lay on the turf weltering in his blood, he was taken away, and the race began again at the appointed time as if nothing had happened.

The brown rider had been the first in the preceding heat, and hoped to win the last and decisive one. It was what the English call 'a hard race'. Both horses and men did their part admirably, they ran and leaped almost in rank. Killarney at last won only by a quarter of a head: it was necessary therefore to run again. This last contest was of course the most interesting, since one of the two running must of necessity win everything. There was a great deal of betting, which at first was even. Twice did the victory appear undecided, and yet at last terminated on the contrary side. At the first leap the horses were together; before they reached the second it was evident that the brown was exhausted, and Killarney gained so much upon him that he reached the second wall more than a hundred paces before him. But here, contrary to all expectations, he refused to leap, and the rider had lost all power over him. Before he could be brought to obey, the brown came up, made his leap well; and now putting out all his strength, was so much ahead that he seemed sure of winning. Bets were now ten to one. But the last wall was yet to cross, and this was fatal to him. The tired animal, who had exhausted his last remaining strength in fast running, tried the leap willingly enough indeed, but had no longer power to effect it; and half breaking down the wall, he rolled bleeding over and over, burying his rider under him, so that it was impossible for him to rise. Killarney's rider had in the meantime brought the refractory horse into subjection, achieved the two remaining leaps amid the cheers of the multitude, and then rode at a foot pace, perfectly at his ease and without a rival, to the goal. He was so exhausted, however, that he could scarcely speak.

In the intervals between the preceding heats I was introduced to many ladies and gentlemen, all of whom most hospitably invited me to their houses.

They wined and dined him in the high style they were accustomed to, while the poor wretches who followed his coach went back to their cabins to survive as best they could until the next races or patron came round to bring respite to their misery. But a nation was stirring again, and due mainly to the efforts of one great man, the people were beginning to assert their rights.

The political struggle would be a long and bitter one, but Máire Ní Laoghaire, the wife of a tenant farmer in West Cork, saw it ending in victory for her people, and in the rout of the English:

Beidh stealladh piléar agus pící géara
Dhá gcur 'na méadail bhrúidigh,
Beidh cloch is craobh orthu ó láimh gach aoinne
Agus mallacht Dé ar a gcomplacht;
Beidh siad faonlag faoi spalladh gréine
Gan neach sa tsaol ina gcúram,
A gcoin 'sa mbéagles is a gcapaill traochta
Gan dúil i ngéim ná i liú acu.

(Flying bullets and sharp pikes shall send them packing; stones and sticks in every man's hands and God's curse on all their company. They may yet be brought down, without a possession in the world: their hounds, their beagles and their horses enervated, with no further interest in hunting and kindred sports.)

The political leadership of a Catholic squire from Uibh Rathach in west Kerry was the cause of this optimism.

THE KING OF THE BEGGARS

Daniel o'connell of Derrynane was fond of quoting this verse composed by a tenant of his, well aware that millions of oppressed people acclaimed him as their hero:

> *Sé Dónall binn Ó Conaill caoin*
> *An planda fíor den Ghael-fhuil;*
> *Gur le foghlaim dlí is meabhair a chinn*
> *Do scól sé síos an craos-shliocht.*

(It was bold Daniel O'Connell, a true son of the Irish race, who, through intellect and a knowledge of law, scalded the oppressors.)

Contrary to their expectation, the Act of Union was not accompanied by a bill designed to remove the civil disabilities under which Catholics suffered; Pitt had intended that under the Union they should be conceded perfect equality of civil rights but George III, guided by public opinion, refused to give his assent to the proposals of his prime minister, on the grounds that to do so would be a violation of his coronation oath.

When O'Connell came on the political scene his people were prevented by religious tests from sitting in parliament and from filling important civil and military positions; neither could they become magistrates or King's Counsels. He changed all that—he gained emancipation after a twenty year struggle.

It matters little that he failed to achieve his other ambition, the repeal of the Union. For his greatest achievement was the revivification of a nation,

The king of the beggars, from Punch

the rekindling of national aspirations in a people he had called, not without some justification, crawling slaves. He had showed them the possibilities of politics; he was, as the American historian, Potter, put it, 'the first modern man to use the mass of a people as a democratic instrument for revolutionary changes by peaceful, constitutional methods. He anticipated the coming into power of the people as the decisive political element in modern democratic society'; and in the Catholic Association which he founded in 1823, he established 'the first fully-fledged democratic political party known to the world'.

Pückler-Muskau met O'Connell a year before emancipation was granted:

AT LENGTH it began to grow dark just as I reached a part of the coast, which assuredly it would be difficult to parallel. Foreign travellers have probably never been thrown into this desolate corner of the earth, which belongs rather to owls and seamews than to men, and of whose awful wildness it is difficult to give an idea. Torn, jagged, coalblack rocks, with deep caverns, into which the sea breaks with a ceaseless thunder, and then again dashes over the top of the tower-like crags its white foam; which, drying, is borne by the wind in compact masses, like locks of wool, over the highest points of the mountains; the wailing cry of the restless fluttering sea-fowl, piercing through the storm with its shrill monotonous sound; the incessant howl and roar of the undermining waves, which sometimes suddenly dashed over my horse's hoofs, and then ran hissing back again; the comfortless removal from all human help; the ceaseless pattering rain, and the coming-on of night on an uncertain and entirely unknown road.

At length, at length a bright light broke through the darkness; the road grew more even; here and there a bit of hedge was visible; and in a few minutes we stopped at the gate of an ancient building standing on the rocky shore, from the windows of which a friendly golden radiance streamed through the night.

The tower clock was striking eleven, and I was, I confess, somewhat anxious as to my dinner, especially as I saw no living being, except a man in a dressing-gown at an upper window. Soon, however, I heard sounds in the house; a handsomely-dressed servant appeared, bearing silver candlesticks, and opened the door of a room, in which I saw with astonishment a company of from fifteen to twenty persons sitting at a long table, on which were placed wine and dessert. A tall handsome man, of cheerful and agreeable aspect, rose to receive me, apologised for having given me up in consequence of the lateness of the hour, regretted that I had made such a journey in such terrible weather, presented me in a cursory manner to his family, who formed the majority of the company, and then conducted me to my bedroom. This was the great O'Connell.

On my return to the dining-room I found the greater part of the company there assembled. I was most hospitably entertained; and it would be ungrateful not to make honourable mention of Mr O'Connell's old and capital wine. As soon as the ladies had quitted us, he drew his seat near me, and Ireland was of course the subject of our conversation. He asked me if I had yet seen many of the curiosities of Ireland? Whether I had been at the Giant's Causeway? 'No,' replied I, laughing, 'before I visit the Giant's Causeway, I wished to see Ireland's Giants'—and therewith drank a glass of claret to his high undertakings.

Daniel O'Connell is indeed no common man, though the man of the commonalty. His power is so great, that at this moment it only depends on him to raise the standard of rebellion from one end of the island to the other. He is, however, too sharp-sighted, and much too sure of attaining his end by safer means, to wish to bring on any such violent crisis. He has certainly shown great dexterity in availing himself of the temper of the country at this moment, legally, openly, and in the face of the government, to acquire a power scarcely inferior to that of the sovereign; indeed, though without arms or armies, in some instances far surpassing it; for how would it have been possible for His Majesty George IV, to withhold forty thousand of his faithful Irishmen for three days from whiskey-drinking—which O'Connell actually accomplished in the memorable Clare election. The enthusiasm of the people rose to such a height that they themselves decreed and inflicted a punishment for drunkenness. The delinquent was thrown into a certain part of the river, and held there for two hours, during which time he was made to undergo frequent submersions.

The next day I had fuller opportunity of observing O'Connell. On the whole, he exceeded my expectations. His exterior is attractive; and the expression of intelligent good nature, united with determination and prudence, which marks his countenance, is extremely winning. He has, perhaps, more

Daniel O'Connell

Daniel O'Connell's address on Repeal

Mr O'Connell's Address on the
REPEAL of the UNION,

of persuasiveness than of genuine large and lofty eloquence; and one frequently perceives too much design and manner in his words. Nevertheless, it is impossible not to follow his powerful arguments with interest, to view the martial dignity of his carriage without pleasure, or to refrain from laughing at his wit. It is very certain that he looks much more like a general of Napoleon's than a Dublin advocate. This resemblance is rendered much more striking by the perfection with which he speaks French, having been educated at the Jesuits' Colleges at Douai and St Omer. His family is old, and was probably one of the great families of the land. His friends, indeed, maintain that he springs from the ancient kings of Kerry, an opinion which no doubt adds to the reverence with which he is regarded by the people. He himself told me, and not without a certain pretension, that one of his cousins was Comte O'Connell, and *cordon rouge* in France, and another a baron, general and chamberlain to the Emperor of Austria; but that he was the head of the family. It appeared to me that he was regarded by the other members of it with almost religious enthusiasm. He is about fifty years old, and in excellent preservation, though his youth was rather wild and riotous.

Among other things he became notorious, about ten years ago, for a duel he fought. The Protestants, to whom his talents early made him formidable, set on a certain Desterre, a bully and fighter by profession, to ride through all the streets of Dublin with a hunting-whip, which, as he declared, he intended to lay on the shoulders of the king of Kerry. The natural consequence was a meeting the next morning, in which O'Connell lodged a bullet in Desterre's heart; Desterre's shot went through his hat. This was his first victory over the Orangemen, which has been followed by so many more important, and, it is to be hoped, will be followed by others more important still.

His desire for celebrity seemed to me boundless; and if he should succeed in obtaining emancipation, of which I have no doubt, his career, so far from being closed, will I think only then properly begin. But the evils of Ireland, and of the constitution of Great Britain generally, lie too deep to be removed by emancipation. To return to O'Connell, I must mention that he has received from nature an invaluable gift for a party-leader: a magnificent voice, united to good lungs and a strong constitution. His understanding is sharp and quick, and his acquirements out of his profession not inconsiderable. With all this, his manners are, as I have said, winning and popular; although somewhat of the actor is perceivable in them, they do not conceal his very high opinion of himself, and are occasionally tinged by what an Englishman would call 'vulgarity'. Where is there a picture entirely without shade!

Although my kind hosts with true Irish hospitality pressed me to stay a week longer for a great festival which is in preparation, and to which a large company is expected, I did not think it right to take this entirely *à la lettre*; besides which I had such a longing after Glengariff, that I did not wish to absent myself from it longer than was necessary for the end I had in view. I therefore took leave of the family this morning, with the sincerest thanks for the friendly welcome they had given me. O'Connell himself escorted me to the boundaries of his demesne, mounted on a large and handsome grey horse, on which he looked more military than ever.

At the ruins of a bridge carried away by the swelling of a mountain stream, O'Connell stopped to take a final leave of me. I could not help expressing to the champion of the rights of his countrymen, my wish that when we next met, the dungeons and fortresses of English intolerance might be overthrown by him and his allies, as completely as these ruined walls had been by the swollen and overflowing torrent. So we parted.

Johann Köhl met O'Connell in the days of the repeal agitation, a few years before the great man's death:

ON MY RETURN to the Irish capital, my first visit was to that man whom every stranger in Dublin must be equally eager to see as he would the Pope, if in Rome—I mean the man whom in Kerry they call king 'by courtesy', or in joke, who was then Lord Mayor of Dublin, who is designated throughout all Ireland the 'immortal' and the 'great agitator', and for whom they have in London so many other names. It is certainly a pleasure to be able to converse for a quarter of an hour with a man so clever, so experienced, so distinguished, talented, and intelligent, and who, within the walls of his own house, is such an agreeable and hospitable host. But I will speak as little of O'Connell in his private capacity as I would of the private character of any other man I became acquainted with. Many individuals are unknown beyond the narrow circle of their private life, and these belong entirely to themselves; others, again, appear on the stage of public life, as actors, as authors, or as statesmen, and thus, in some measure, lay themselves open to criticism. Such men, so long as they wear the costume of the part they have assumed, it is allowable to judge, and speak of freely and openly, without committing any breach of decorum. Nay, one may even be their determined public enemy, and at the same time be their sincere friend in private, or at least feel no further hostility towards them.

O'Connell, in proportion as he has made himself public, has retained less of himself for himself than any other man in England. He everywhere gives himself up to the gaze and judgement of the public, whether in parliament or at public meetings, in the streets, at elections, or in travelling. He scarcely ever ceases to lead a public life, and almost everything he does is done before the eyes of hundreds or thousands. Peel, Wellington, and other great statesmen, hide themselves in the mysteries of their bureaux and cabinets, from which they issue forth in their public measures, and in person only in parliament, or at public dinners. O'Connell, the tribune of the people, is almost public property, flesh and bone; he even speaks of his domestic concerns at his popular meetings, for he is enabled to support his house and his family only through the indirect assistance of the public.

Whoever travels in Germany, or in any other country, for geographical or ethnographical purposes, and wishes only to make himself acquainted with the character of the country and its inhabitants, need not trouble himself much about the personal characteristics of our distinguished men. To travel in Ireland for the same purposes, and to remain ignorant of O'Connell, the man who, as Atlas supports the earth, has taken the entire emerald isle on his shoulders, is next to impossible; for he is himself an ethnographical phenomenon, partly because for thirty years he has exercised an extraordinary influence over the formation of the character and the condition of his nation, and partly because he himself and his power is another phenomenon which can only be explained by the character of the Irish nationality.

The Irish are a people after the old model, a people almost without a counterpart in the world. In Germany, we have everywhere become too enlightened and too self-dependent for any authority. We laugh at all who call themselves prophets; but among the Irish the old faith in saints and miracles still exists. Here alone the mighty, the immortal, and the great still find a fertile soil, whence to obtain laurels and a halo. The Irish are enthusiastic, credulous, blind, innocent as children, and patriotic, so that they are ready to abandon themselves to the most ardent admiration of a talented individual,

87

Daniel O'Connell at a Repeal meeting

and to raise him aloft on their shields and shoulders, as the Romans were wont to elevate their generals. They are also unhappy, and desirous to be relieved from their sufferings, and their full, wounded hearts are consequently ever ready to applaud and shower down praises on him who manifests sympathy in their wrongs and devotion in their cause.

In a well-regulated state, among an enlightened, well-groomed people, where everyone possesses some knowledge, and where everyone has sufficient for his waste, the elevation of such a tribune of the people would be a pure impossibility. It was not till Rome's *infima plebs* began to sink in misery and vice, that the tribunes of the people made their appearances on the stage. In Ireland, there are more miserable poor beings, without rights and without property, than in any other country in the world: and it is therefore a soil suited for the production of talented, active, eloquent tribunes like O'Connell. For thirty years has O'Connell represented the vigorous and unwearied arm of Ireland, which, during the whole of that period, has been threatening England, and with which she is again wresting her plundered natural rights, one after the other, from the flames of an English parliament lighted to consume them.

Köhl went to see O'Connell in action at a repeal meeting:

88

THEN AROSE Dan himself, and adjusted his wig. In the heat of his speech he often accidentally touches his wig, sometimes pushing it off a little, and then pulling it down again into its proper position on the other side. It is said that he even took off this wig at a public meeting and exhibited his bald head. On the occasion alluded to he had severely criticised the conduct of a gentleman of the party opposed to him, and, indulging in witticisms on his appearance, had given him to understand that he was not the most handsome man in Dublin. This gentleman replied, that so far as beauty or ugliness was concerned, he believed Dan owed all his beauty to his wig, and that if he were to take it off he would perhaps be still uglier than the speaker. At this the people began to laugh, and looked at O'Connell for his reply. Dan did not take long to consider, but actually took off his wig, and exposed his bald head, at the same time remarking, that as his opponent wished to see his bare head, he was ready to favour him with a view of it; it had become bald in the service of his country, and therefore he was neither ashamed nor sorry for it; whilst his fellow-countrymen would feel greater pleasure in seeing his uncovered head, bald and ugly as it might be, than with the wig on it. By this ready tact, and the fearless, frank disregard of himself thus displayed, he turned the laughter and the sympathy of the audience to his own side.

Besides this manoeuvre with the wig, he indulges in some other little habits while speaking. For instance, he hops or turns about on his heels as on a pivot, and even jumps up with his whole body. Every standing speaker, I believe, does this more or less, though not at such regular intervals as O'Connell. In the French chamber of deputies there are individuals, especially persons of small stature, who at certain emphatic parts of their speeches raise themselves on the extreme tips of their toes, and stand thus for a long time, as if they would fly after their own fervent words. With O'Connell, however, as I have said, the motion is rather a little jumping and turning about on his heels. Even his son does the same, probably through involuntary imitation of his father. With this movement, O'Connell is for ever slightly changing his position, so that if he were previously facing the left side of the assembly, after a few moments he turns his face towards the right, and after another short interval he again turns round. There appeared to me something mechanical and automatical in this constant twisting and turning of his person. While speaking, he also makes great use of his hands, in order to give increased

89

King O'Connell at Tara, from Punch

emphasis to his words, sometimes striking the table, or any other object near him. On the present occasion the arm of the president's chair was thus operated upon, and in order to devote it more entirely to O'Connell's service, the person by whom it was occupied had squeezed himself up into one corner of his seat.

Although O'Connell's language is very clear and precise, still he does not speak so fluently as his son: he sometimes hesitates, thinks, and repeats himself: but all this ceases when he becomes warm and enthusiastic. What struck me most, was that he possessed so much of the Irish brogue. He did not, it is true, say *repale*, like Tom Steele, and some others who were present; but he pronounced the English 'th' almost like 'd', as, for example, 'de wishes', with some other Irish peculiarities of accent. This brogue is so difficult to be lost, that the most refined Irishmen always retain a portion of it, which is very unpleasant to English ears; and it is said that even the Duke of Wellington cannot wholly divest himself of it.

Köhl witnessed the collection of a repeal tribute and came to the conclusion that O'Connell was motivated by monetary considerations as well as by patriotism. He remarked:

WE MUST ALSO consider O'Connell as a child of our own age, and in this respect make great allowances for his conduct. It is possible, it is even probable, that if, like J. J. Rousseau, he had refused the assistance of his friends, if, like Cincinnatus, he had lived by the plough—or if, like the millions of his poor compatriots, he had clothed himself in rags, and subsisted on nothing but potatoes, he might never have attained such power, but, on the contrary, have been despised and neglected by the people. Perhaps the present age will and must have its heroes well dressed and well fed. As the English national debt is a burden which keeps all England together, so is the O'Connell tribute a burden which keeps together all repealers. Having once pledged themselves to pay so much, this promise obliges them to continue with O'Connell. They are probably astonished at the extraordinary amount of this tribute, which a man without any external power, and merely by his eloquence and zeal, has imposed upon them, and perhaps they value him the more highly on that account. Add to this, that O'Connell is an extraordinary man—a man of authority, power and wealth, by means and ways hitherto unheard of in the world: and who, without employing any physical force, and without making any concessions, has for forty years raised an opposition against the most powerful aristocracy in Europe; while, on his side, he has had almost nothing but a few millions of beggars as supporters.

DRINKING AND LEARNING

MANY OF the travellers, having come to the conclusion that an innate indolence was as much the cause of Ireland's poverty as England's misrule, considered whiskey public enemy number one. The Reverend Theobald Mathew, the Apostle of Temperance, became therefore, in their eyes, a man even greater than O'Connell—a virtual miracle worker. Fr Mathew's influence had penetrated into the most remote districts of the country, as John Barrow found out when he visited 'the houseless wilds of Connemara' in 1835:

ON THE POTEEN being produced I hoped Big Jack Joyce would not oblige me to drink alone; but it was not without much entreaty I could prevail upon him to take a single glass, which he did only, he said, to welcome my arrival. *Tempora mutantur*, thought I, and some of us are changed with them; for it was scarcely a twelve-month since Inglis visited him, when 'room was found on the table for a double-sized flagon of whiskey, and water appeared to be a beverage not much in repute'. The mystery was soon unriddled by his telling me that he—Joyce, of all men in the world—had become a member of a temperance society! and had taken a vow (on three months trial) not to drink spirits, save and except on such an occasion as the present, and when necessary to do so medicinally. He, however, gave me to understand that he had taken his fair share of poteen in his day, and was nothing the worse of it.

It is to be hoped that this honest fellow will not endeavour to prevail on his poor neighbours to forego entirely this necessary beverage; absolutely

One for the road, from a painting by Erskine Nicol

Father Mathew's total abstinence pledge

necessary, as I am assured by a medical gentleman of great eminence, to prevent scorbutic habits in those whose chief or sole food is the potato, which Cobbett not improperly calls 'the root of poverty'. Rice has not much more nutrition in it than potatoes, and yet the millions of India and China feed upon little else; they never eat it alone; it is either dressed in the shape of curries, or highly seasoned with pepper and other hot spices, which answers the purpose of whiskey.

Barrow was an exception in extolling the virtues of poteen; even Pückler-Muskau, who loved the stuff, thought that the Irish drank far too much of it. Mrs Hall suggested that the singing of drinking-songs be prohibited in whiskey shops; she was appalled at the character of some of them, especially those that glorified the champion drinkers.

Father Mathew had his work cut out for him, but he did wonders in weaning the Irish from their worst habit. All over the country distilleries shut down and hundreds of thousands came forward to take the pledge.

Thackeray met people who assured him that all the fun had gone out of Ireland since Father Mathew banished the whiskey from it; and the Englishman admitted that as a stranger going among the people he found them anything but gay. There was now no merriment as there was in what he called 'the pleasant but wrong old times for which one can't help having an antiquarian fondness'.

Köhl, on the other hand, was convinced that Father Mathew was the saviour of the Irish nation:

IT MAY BE doubted whether history furnishes an example of so great a moral revolution, accomplished in so short a time, and whether any man ever so quickly obtained so great and bright a name as Father Mathew. In point of fact, there is something altogether unparalleled in the Irish Temperance Society . . . where is to be found a similar example of a people, wholly without preparation, without previous instruction, rising unanimously at the call of a single individual, in the very plenitude of their vices (for the Irish were the greatest and the most habitual drunkards in the world) contending against itself, against its own passions (not against the privileged classes, or its powerful priesthood), tearing up sweet old habits by the roots, and confining itself to strict and rigorous abstinence! Here is an entire people doing what, in the middle ages, but a few pious monks were able to accomplish! How hard it is to fulfil that saying of Christ, that we should put off the old man and put on the new! Yet here we see the wonderful phenomenon of five millions of men fulfilling this command in one particular. They have put off an old man, worn out with diseases which have hitherto resisted the medicine of every physician, and have suddenly put on a new, vigorous, abstinent, and sober man . . .

The people flocked together passionately, even madly, by thousands, nay by hundreds of thousands, and allowed themselves to be converted by the great Apostle, whose glorious triumph has scarcely ever been equalled. In one day Father Mathew frequently admitted from four to eight thousand

and upon one occasion thirteen thousand persons, into the Temperance Society. On his first visit to Galway, no fewer than two hundred thousand individuals flocked together to see and hear him, and, for the most part, to be enrolled on the list of teetotalism. As the Irish Temperance Society has been five years in existence, and as it now numbers five millions of members, it must, on an average, have received nearly three thousand daily. These are extraordinary occurrences, for which the historian can hardly find a parallel; and the affair is more honourable to the Irish nation than anything else that has hitherto been known of it . . .

Father Mathew's eloquence is one of these endowments for which he is particularly admired. In point of fact, he possesses a sonorous voice, and what is much more important, a glowing enthusiasm, and a firm conviction of the success of the cause. He occasionally hesitates, and even stammers. After he has been speaking for some time quite fluently and rapidly, he seems all at once unable to find some suitable word, or to express an idea sufficiently quick. His speech stops short, his tongue no longer obeys him, the construction of his sentences becomes entangled, his thoughts grow confused, he stops for a moment, he grows red, his regularly beautiful countenance becomes even distorted, he begins to make some convulsive efforts, and to help out his meaning with some movements of his hands, till at length the knot is suddenly unloosed, the thoughts again begin to flow, the new idea is born, the tongue again recovers its volubility, and the speech rushes along, sonorous and copious as before. I believe that this stopping and hesitation, which might seem to be a defect in an orator, often increases the interest with which Father Mathew is listened to.

Köhl was present at a tea-party given in Father Mathew's honour. The speeches lasted well into the small hours, but the energetic priest was hard at work again at nine o'clock the following morning.

THIS TIME, however, the scene of his labours was the church, where he read Mass, and then distributed temperance medals to some hundreds of persons who presented themselves for that purpose. This medal is a round piece of pewter, about the size of a five-franc piece. Upon it are stamped the words of the pledge, which are to the effect that the holder will abstain from all intoxicating liquors, and do all in his power to dissuade others from using them. Some persons, as I have said, wear them constantly as a kind of amulet. They frequently hang them round the necks of their children, who are admitted into the society long before they know anything of intoxicating liquors, evidently for the same reason that the Russians and other nations cause the sacrament to be administered to their children, before they know anything of its significance. The wealthy have silver medals, which they wear on festive occasions. Along with this medal each person receives a paper, a sort of diploma, or certificate of admission into the society. In Ireland this medal is called 'the pledge', and to 'take the pledge' means the same as to become a member of the society. On the other hand, to 'break the pledge' means to break the vow, and again return to intemperance. This of course is frequently the case, and it is not unusual to hear expressions of regret that so many have broken the pledge. Nor is this surprising. On the contrary, it is a wonder that so many millions conscientiously and faithfully confine themselves within the narrow bounds to which the temperance pledge confines them. It often happens that individuals come to Father Mathew with repentant confessions, return him their broken pledge, and entreat him to administer it once more. This he usually does, after inflicting on them some slight ecclesiastical punishment for breaking their vow. Frequently too, people give him back the pledge, and entreat him entirely to release them from their vow, which circumstances make it impossible for them to keep.

There are numbers also, who have manifold ways of evading their vow. Many, I was informed, allege that they only pledged themselves not to drink intoxicating liquors in any wine, beer or whiskey shop, but they may fill their glass in the house and drink it on the street. Such cases may occur, but they are, I have little doubt, extremely rare. Father Mathew himself related to me a strange case of an old colonel, who was much tormented by the gout. He had not personally taken the pledge, but two of his sons were teetotallers. He sometimes used to resolve, probably when he was suffering from his disorder, to devote himself to temperance. At such times he would borrow a medal from one of his sons, and wear it as an amulet to counteract his wish for intoxicating liquors. But no sooner had the gout disappeared than his love for the bottle again returned, and the medal was forthwith returned to his

A hedge-school, c. 1840

son. As long, however, as he wore it, he strictly refrained from drinking a single drop; and his conduct in the matter may be regarded as not a little characteristic of the manner in which the Irish frequently appreciate both the medal and the pledge.

An saol bocht—the poor times—the Kerry poet, Tomás Rua Ó Súilleabháin, called those pre-famine days. Tomás was not a disciple of Father Mathew, and in one of his songs he longed for an Ireland where the landlord class would be deprived of its drink and their cellars opened to the country's poor. Tomás was a hedge schoolmaster, one of the last of the men who had provided a truly national, non-sectarian education from Cromwellian times. During the penal days of the eighteenth century the wandering schoolmasters gave their pupils a classical education in wretched hovels built against the sides of ditches; in the first decades of the new century the hedge schools outnumbered all other schools and they continued to be so profoundly national that the government hastened to introduce, in 1831, a state system of education. Tomás Rua Ó Súilleabháin taught in a hovel in west Kerry, and he described his schoolhouse in verse:

Tá tigh scoile beag theas i nDrom Caor agam,
Láimh le loch aerach an ghrinn
Bíonn scoláirí na háite go léir ann
'S ó gach baile ón dtaobh eile de'n tír.
Nuair a thagann an bháisteach on spéir chugainn
Crádhann agus céasann mo chroí,
Is do thánas ag cásamh mo ghaolta
D'iarraidh ádhbhairín éigin den tuí!

(I have a little schoolhouse near Drom Caor, beside a sparkling lake. The scholars come both from that place and from the surrounding countryside as well. When the rain falls, it persecutes me near to heartbreak; and I must go among my friends begging a little straw to thatch the roof.)

The emphasis was laid on mathematics and the classics in the hedge schools. Many distinguished nineteenth-century academics owed all to them and acknowledged the debt, among them James Thomson, who became Professor of Mathematics in Glasgow University, and James McCullagh who entered Trinity College, Dublin, from a hedge school and was appointed professor of mathematics in 1836, at the age of twenty-five. Some of the hedge school-masters lived on to teach in the national schools, and many of those who did refused to be confined to the syllabus approved by the Board. Tommy Maher had for years taught in a mud hut at Goffs Bridge in county Wexford, and for this reason the Board of Education sent an inspector to examine his pupils when he transferred his allegiance to it in 1835. The Archdeacon of Ferns received his report in due course. The inspector wrote:

AMAZED AT the skill of the twelve
year old boys in reading the new books, and considering the possibility that
they were reciting from memory, I invited one of their number to read me
a passage from the Gospel of Saint Matthew. Evidently the child misunderstood me. He searched in his satchel until he found his tattered book, stood
up, and proceeded to read me the account of Christ's passion—in Greek.

Johann Köhl visited one of the last of the old hedge schools during his stay
in Ireland:

AN IRISH HEDGE school which I visited
—one in the pure old national style—enabled me to observe the mode by
which, in these remote parts of Ireland, the light of intellectual cultivation is
transmitted. It was, in truth, a touching sight. The schoolhouse was a mud
hovel, covered with green sods, without windows or any other comforts.
The little pupils, wrapped up as well as their rags would cover them, sat
beside the low open door, towards which they were all holding their books
in order to obtain a portion of the scanty light it admitted. Some of the
younger ones were sitting or lying on the floor; behind these, others were
seated on a couple of benches formed of loose boards; and behind these again
stood taller children, also holding their books towards the light between the
heads of the front rank. The master, dressed in the national costume already
described, was seated in the midst of the crowd. In a sketch-book of Ireland
this would be an essential picture, and I regret that I had not a Daguerreotype
with me to perpetuate the scene. Outside, before the door, lay as many pieces
of turf as there were scholars within, for each one had brought a piece with
him as a fee or gratuity for the schoolmaster. The latter, as I entered the narrow
door, rose from a barrel and saluted me in a friendly manner: 'Indeed, I am
very sorry, your honour,' said he, 'that I am not able to offer you a chair.'
He was teaching the children the English alphabet, and they all appeared very
cheerful, smart and bright-eyed over their study. When their poverty, their
food, and clothing are considered, this may appear surprising; but it is the
case with all Irish children, and especially those in the open country. The
school-house stood close by the roadside, but many of the children resided
several miles off, and even the schoolmaster did not live near it. At a certain
hour they all met here; and when the day's task is over the boys put their

primers in their pockets and scamper off home; whilst the schoolmaster fastens the door as well as he can, puts his turf fees into his bag, takes his stick and trudges off to his remote cottage across the bog.

Before the introduction of state education, the hedge schools were the only places where Catholic children could receive a schooling free from real, or imagined, proselytising. Charter schools, whose purpose was to give poor Catholic children an industrial education and to convert them to Protestantism, existed since 1733. Although they were found all over the country, the number of Catholic children attending them was small. 'To account for this', said the Halls,

IT WILL BE necessary only to extract a few pages from the Catechism in use in all these schools, at least until within a comparatively recent period.

A hedge-school

A holy well in rural Ireland

Q: Is the Church of Rome a sound and uncorrupt Church?
A: No; it is extremely corrupt in doctrine, worship and practice.
Q: What do you think of the frequent crossings, upon which the papists lay so great a stress in their divine offices and for security against sickness and all accidents?
A: They are vain and superstitious. The worship of the crucifix, or figure of Christ upon the cross, is idolatrous; and the adoring and praying to the cross itself is, of all the corruptions of the papish worship, the most gross and intolerable.

In 1815 Peel succeeded in procuring a state grant for elementary education.

This grant was administered by the Kildare Place Society, a non-denominational body which supported schools throughout Ireland. But, as the Halls explained, an opinion largely prevailed among the Roman Catholics that their secret paramount object was to proselytise, an opinion that received weight from the over-zealous and most injudicious conduct of some of the members, and so these schools found little favour with the Catholic hierarchy. By 1825, however, several religious orders were at work, among them the Christian Brothers, the Presentation Sisters and the Ursulines. By 1831 the payment of the Kildare Place Society grant had become such a bone of contention that it was handed over to a new board, the Commissioners for National Education. The government policy was to provide 'a system of education from which should be banished even the suspicion of proselytism, and which, admitting children of all religious persuasions, should not interfere with the peculiar tenets of any'. Joint secular and separate religious instruction was the basis of the new system. It was distrusted by the Catholic hierarchy and the Church of Ireland and was attacked strongly by the Presbyterians. Within a generation these three religious groups were running their own schools within the system. Johann Köhl, who cared nothing for Irish national aspirations, was quite impressed by what he saw in one of them in 1842.

IN WEXFORD I paid a visit to one of the many hundreds of infant schools which are now established all over England and Ireland. The schools are at present particularly interesting in Ireland, as both Roman Catholic and Protestant children meet together in them, evincing that not only is greater toleration shown towards each other by the two parties, but that, by means of these schools, a still greater degree of toleration will be produced. The one I visited at Wexford, like most of the Irish infant schools, had only been established five years, and contained ninety-one Catholic and thirty Protestant children. The children usually remain until their twelfth year, but the Catholics often send their daughters back again, as they are dissatisfied with the parochial schools which are attended by those of more advanced age. The Protestant children seldom return, better schools being provided for them. The system of education at these infant schools is very peculiar, and, indeed, extremely poetical. All the instruction is conveyed in verses, which are sung by the little pupils, and, whenever it is

103

possible, accompanied with a pantomimic acting of the subject. Almost every general movement made by the children is attended with singing. For instance, as they come into the school-room they sing the following verse:

We'll go to our places, and make no wry faces,
And say all our lessons distinctly and slow;
For if we don't do it, our mistress will know it,
And into the corner we surely shall go.

When I entered the school all the little things were in the garden. At the sound of their teacher's bell they immediately took each other's hands, and marched two by two, in a long procession, into the school-room, singing the song of which the above is a portion. I recognised the air as the 'Infants' March', an old British national melody which I had frequently heard in Ireland. They all looked very cheerful and shrieked to their hearts' content; and even the tiny beings of three years old, who did not know how to join the song, opened their mouths as wide as if they were going to be fed with peaches. What joyousness must not this singing entrée of the little ones immediately spread over the entire school! As they all march in procession, everyone hastens to join the great train; no-one stays behind, and there is no chiding reception at the door. The mistress, indeed, has no time to spare for chiding, for she herself accompanies the little ones in their song. The instruction principally consists in learning and repeating these verses. Thus they have the multiplication table in verse, a natural history in verse, and an A B C in verse; and the mistress, while repeating the verses, points out the letter or the picture of the animal she is describing. The pictures now used in all English schools, even in these infant schools, are well drawn; and as each ox, lion or elephant, or each A, X or Z is exhibited to the children, they sing a verse.

A kind of pantomimic action, accompanied with singing, is also frequently used; and in this manner all those occupations of men which can possibly be imitated by the hands and feet, are represented by the children. The sowing and reaping of the husbandman, the planing of the carpenter, the hammering of the smith, the churning of the dairy-maid, are all imitated, the children at the same time singing, 'this is the way the carpenter planes', 'this is the way we snuff the candle', 'this is the way we churn the butter'. Some remarks are afterwards made on every subject, as, for what purpose the board is planed—why the candle must be carefully snuffed—how good bread and butter tastes, and that if they have any to spare they should give it to those who have none. I have never seen these rhymes except in manuscript, and the teachers informed me some of them were composed by themselves, and some they copied from the collections of others. It is probable, however, that there are printed collections of them which chanced not to fall into my hands.

Many objects are accomplished at the same time by this combination of pantomime and song. In the first place, the attention of the children is directed to a multitude of occurrences and occupations that are going on around them, and which they are thus led to imitate; and as children generally possess a strong disposition for this imitation, it is by this means assisted and developed. Being all more or less intended for artisans, labourers, sempstresses, dairy-maids, and similar employments, their arms are thus exercised and trained, as it were, for those industrious occupations which they are hereafter to follow. The recollection of it will also throw a more cheerful light upon their future hours of labour, when they are actually engaged in that which they only imitated in their youth, in the midst of their playmates, and accompanied

A class in the schoolyard, late nineteenth century

by their song. These pantomimes afford a wholesome relaxation from a long sitting posture, as during their performance the children are standing up and in motion; and lastly, they exercise both the voice and the ear. As the mistress has not time to teach these verses to each child singly, they must in a great degree teach themselves. The youngest at first only open their mouths, or imitate the motions of the hands; they then learn to sing some of the principal words and catch some of the rhymes and notes. To these rhymes the whole verse is gradually added; and finally, from the verse the clear conception and the fruitful idea began to dawn on their minds. This practice of embellishing instruction by poetry and learning, and by committing verses to memory, is a favourite mode of teaching in England, and is everywhere practised, from these infant schools up to Eton College and other academies, and is regarded as a very practical method of teaching. As many very young children attend the infant schools to whom this instruction for hours together would be too fatiguing, a bed, on which the wearied are put to rest, is part of the usual furniture of the school-room.

The national school system was totally out of touch with the aspirations of the majority of the Irish people. The verses that used to be recited daily by the school children tell their own tale:

> *I thank the goodness and the grace*
> *That on my birth have smiled,*
> *And made me in these Christian days*
> *A happy English child.*

In these schools the Irish language was proscribed and along with famine, emigration and the neglect of native churchmen and politicians, the schools are blamed for the language's decline. In 1831 the number of people who regarded Irish as their mother tongue was probably in the region of one and a half millions (the estimate made by the German historian Lappenberg of four millions in 1835 is generally regarded as being wildly inaccurate) and even in the northern counties great numbers of people could, in the early days of national education, be found who spoke Irish. In her book *Letters from Ireland*, published in 1838, Charlotte Elizabeth Tonna, a missionary whose picturesque maledictions on popery led to her *opera omnia* being placed on the Roman Index, found that in county Down the native language prevailed to a much greater extent than she supposed possible, and she mentions that it was necessary for the missionaries to distribute Irish testaments in many country districts. After fifty years of national education the number of people who claimed to speak only Irish declined to sixty-four thousand.

A little encouragement from the commissioners for national education might have saved the language: Johann Köhl found that it still survived in some of Leinster's towns in 1842:

DROGHEDA IS a very Irish town—the last genuine Irish one the traveller meets with on this coast as he advances northwards, for after it, everything is more inclined to the Scotch. Nay, Drogheda is perhaps more Irish than many a town in the south or west of the island. Many persons are to be found in the neighbourhood who understand and speak the old Irish language, and say that they cannot speak English with comfort and fluency. Nay, according to what I was told by the inhabitants, I must believe that the Irish language is far more general in and about Drogheda than at any other point of the eastern coast of Ireland.

As I was now about to take leave of the old Celtic soil, all these matters combined to render me more desirous to be present at an Irish poetical musical soirée.

The first person who came forward was an Irish declaimer, a man from among the people—I know not whether a gardener, a ploughman, or a 'broken farmer', but I was told he knew a countless number of old Irish poems and songs. He came in and thus addressed me: 'Out of friendship for him (meaning the priest) I am come: he told me that there was a foreigner here who wished to hear some of our old Irish poems, and I will gladly recite to him what I know.'

'I am much obliged to you', said the priest, 'but if you were to recite all you know, we would be obliged to listen to you all night, and perhaps many other nights besides.'

'It is true our forefathers have handed down to us a great number of poems from generation to generation; and very beautiful ones they are too, sir, if you could only understand them. How beautiful is not the song of

107

Old town-gate, Drogheda

Tobar a t-Solais, that is, of the glittering spirit, which is but three miles distant from our town; or that of Cuchullin, the Irish champion. Shall I begin with the song of Cuchullin, your reverence?'

'Do, my son, and God bless you!'

The man began to declaim, and recited for a quarter of an hour without stopping.

I, of course, did not understand a single word of all this recitation, but

108

my host was kind enough to relate the story to me afterwards. To understand, however, was not so much my object as to convince myself, by my own ears, that this old Ossianic poetry is still living and extant here in Ireland among the people. The recitater was, as I have said, a simple man, and his recitation was as simple, unadorned, and undeclamatory as himself. Sometimes, however, when carried away by the beauty of the poetry and the ideas, he became animated, and even appeared much affected; he would then look at his hearers as if he expected their sympathy and admiration for himself and his poem. Sometimes I remarked that the metre of the poem changed, and I was told that this was the case in all their poems, and that the metre always adapted itself to the subject. On the battlefield the father and the son had a dialogue which they said was the most beautiful part of the whole poem, but that they could give me no idea of it, for when translated into prose it would lose all its sublimity; and that I, being unacquainted with the language, could form as little idea of it through the medium of any other language as a blind man of the splendour of the sun . . .

The harp was produced, and a blind young harper prepared to play some old Irish pieces. I was told that he was one of the most distinguished harp players in the surrounding country, and, in fact, his music enraptured us all . . . While the Irish listen to these old airs and think of these old deeds, and while their hearts beat at the recollection of their former glory, their present slavery rises up before them, and they perhaps look forward into a free and glorious future, with the same feelings as they look back towards a once glorious past . . .

After Brian Boru's march followed the air of *The Fairy Queen,* a very old Irish piece, as I was told. This much I can say, that it was quite a charming composition—so soft, so enchanting, and so wild, sportive, and playful withal, that during its performance I could think of nothing but the dancing of fairies and the singing of elves. I afterwards heard it several times on the piano, but on that instrument the music was far from being so soft and rich as from the harp of this blind young minstrel. Although the second part of our evening's entertainment, which was given in a language universally intelligible, afforded me much more enjoyment than the first, I am less able to describe it; since, of all the arts, music is that of whose wonderful production the aesthetic critic is least able to convey an adequate idea by description or criticism.

A home in Connemara, late nineteenth century

One of the company assured me that he possessed hundreds of beautiful old songs and poems in manuscript, which had long been hereditary in his family, and not a single one of which has ever been printed.

The manuscripts, carefully though families preserve them as precious heirlooms, are daily becoming less numerous. The memory of the people, faithful and strong as it may be, without doubt loses every year more and more of the beautiful old verses. And besides, the number of those who can value these verses, enjoy and learn them, is visibly growing smaller; for the English language is spreading with strides ever increasing in rapidity, while the Irish is retiring before it into the more remote wilds.

As regards higher education, Trinity College was the only university in the country until the new Queen's College began admitting students in 1849. Trinity's gates were open to all, but both Catholics and Presbyterians strongly resented its Anglican character. It was expensive as well, and consequently its degrees were closed to all but the rich.

In the last decade of the eighteenth century there had been a strong lobby in favour of educating Irish Catholic students for the priesthood at Trinity. Before the French Revolution these clerical students had been educated abroad, but the hierarchy feared that any further contact with continental Europe might subject them to the 'contagion of sedition and infidelity'. The proposal to educate the students in Trinity was disregarded and in 1796 the Royal College of St Patrick in Maynooth was established. Many of the travellers in early nineteenth-century Ireland disliked the seminary, its outlook and its inmates. Thackeray described it in 1842:

OF THE CATHOLIC college at Maynooth, I must likewise speak briefly, for the reason that an accurate description of that establishment would be of necessity so disagreeable that it is best to pass it over in a few words. An Irish poorhouse is a palace to it. Ruin so needless, filth so disgusting, such a look of lazy squalor, no Englishman who has not seen can conceive. Lecture room and dining hall, kitchen and student's room were all the same. I shall never forget the sight of scores of shoulders of mutton lying on the filthy floor in the former, or the view of a bed and dressing-table that I saw in the other. Let the next Maynooth grant include a few shillings-worth of whitewash, and a few hundredweight of soap; and if to this be added a half score of drill sergeants to see that the students appear clean at lectures, and to teach them to keep their heads up and to look people in the face, parliament will introduce some cheap reforms into the seminary which were never needed more than here. Why should the place be so shamefully ruinous and so foully dirty? Lime is cheap, and water plenty at the canal hard by . . . I hope these words will not be taken hostilely.

They were, of course, resented somewhat. So were the opinions of Henry Inglis who visited the college in 1834. He remarked:

I HAD AMPLE opportunity of forming comparisons between the priest of the olden times and the priest of May-nooth: and, with every disposition to deal fairly by both, I did return to Dublin with a perfect conviction of the justice of the opinion which I had heard expressed. I found the old foreign-educated priest a gentleman; a man of frank, easy deportment and good general information; but by no means,

in general, so good a Catholic as his brother of Maynooth: he, I found either
a coarse vulgar-minded man, or a stiff, close and very conceited man.

Eight years later Mr and Mrs Hall found the college at Maynooth not to their
liking. They observed:

THE LEADING objections to the system
pursued at Maynooth are, in brief, these: the amount of knowledge required
at entrance is limited in quantity and far from being good in quality; the
course of study is narrow in its range; dogmatic theology occupies too large
a portion of it, physical science is very lightly touched on, and the course of
metaphysics and ethics is not suited to the present state of mental and moral
science. The discipline is perfectly monastic: it is the iron rule of St Bernard
revived in the nineteenth century. The cultivation of *belles lettres* and general
literature is discouraged, if not actually prohibited. The professors are not
appointed by open competition and public examination. The college should
be, undoubtedly, removed from the miserable village where it at present
stands, to the immediate neighbourhood of some city where, while the
students are subjected to wholesome and sufficient restraint, they may be
permitted occasional intercourse with mankind, instead of being, as they are
at present, as completely immured from society as if they had taken monastic
vows. The college might be placed under Dublin University, and its students
be obliged to present themselves twice in the year at the terminal examinations
in Trinity.

Maynooth, in its early years, was far from national in its outlook, and this
fact did not go unnoticed by many of those who came to Ireland in those
years. Kohl found the attitude of the clergy of Cork city towards the poor
contemptible, and it seems that the fortunes of the Irish language did not
greatly interest the city's clergy in 1842. The German remarked:

IN FOLLOWING UP the complete
emancipation of the Catholics and the reforming of their situation, it is to be

hoped that the position of their priests may speedily be altered, so as to do away with the contemptible practices which still prevail in their churches. I allude more especially to the collections which are made at the doors of Catholic churches for the benefit of the priesthood; the small income of the Irish priests has compelled them to collect a tribute from church-goers, for the service of God, such as is not raised in a similar manner in any other Catholic country. I witnessed these collections in several places, among others in Cork. The tribute was gathered at two entrances—at the principal gate where the poor went into the Church and were obliged to pay a penny each; and at a side door where the rich entered, and paid as much more as they pleased. At the latter was posted up, in large letters, *A Silver Collection is Expected*: that is to say, you are expected to pay at least sixpence. A priest attended in person to receive the money, and also, as I was told, to produce by his presence a still more effectual impression on the purses of the people. He returned thanks with a bow for every gift that was deposited on the plate. Before the principal door of the Church, which was open, and on the steps leading to it, were crowded many poor people and beggars—too poor to pay the required tribute. They lay with folded hands and bended knees upon the stones, and listened for the far-off sounds that reached them from the interior of the Church. 'They are satisfied', said my companion, 'if they but hear the little bell of the assistant of the priest who officiates at the altar; when they have heard that little bell from within, and bowed and crossed themselves, they think they have heard Mass and participated in the worship of God.'

I, and many others, who were accustomed to the matter, looked on this scene without perceiving in it anything very disgraceful; but if we examine it narrowly, clearly and sharply, with the torch which Christ has placed in our hands, can we find language too strong in which to reprobate a state of things which forces the priest to resort to such measures in order to support his existence? It is said that the incomes of the Catholic priests in Ireland are chiefly derived from these collections, which are censured by the Protestants still more than by the Catholic laity, although the former are not called on to pay anything, but are in reality those by whom this scandal was originated, since it was by the Protestants that the Irish Catholic Church was deprived of its ancient revenues. The utterly destitute Irish are thus entirely excluded from the worship of God, except what pertains to the tinkling sound of the

Mass bell; and were the inmost recesses of their hearts less deeply imbued with religious feeling the result would be most unfavourable to their spiritual welfare.

Those who deem the ancient Irish language as their mother tongue are still worse provided for. In the great city of Cork—around which Irish is still much spoken—two preachers only deliver sermons in language, and yet it is very natural that the people should wish to hear what they hold most sacred in the language they love the best. A short time since, as I was informed by the chaplain himself, the prisoners in the Cork County Gaol petitioned him occasionally to preach his sermon in Irish instead of English.

Many of the tourists paid tribute to the Irish road-makers and expressed their indebtedness to Signor Bianconi whose coaches most of them used on their travels into the country's more remote regions. Before Bianconi set up his coaching system in 1815 the public conveyances were confined to a few mail and day coaches on the great lines of roads. In parts less frequented by wealthy travellers, particularly from the country places to the market towns, there were no facilities for speedy or convenient communications. The poor had to travel on foot with their burdens, and a farmer living twenty miles from his market town might spend a day riding there, a day doing business and a third day in returning.

Bianconi, born in northern Italy, was sent to London as a youth to avoid conscription, but through some mischance his ship berthed at Dublin, not London. He found employment in a little shop on the quays and was sent out to the country selling religious bric-à-brac. In 1806 he lived in Carrick-on-Suir and afterwards in Clonmel, where he set up shop and got married. James Macaulay, a geologist who travelled the country on a tour of observation when Bianconi was an old man, met the Italian and gave the following account of his enterprise:

IN JULY 1815, he started a car for conveying passengers at cheap rates from Clonmel to Cahir, and soon after to Tipperary and Limerick. At the end of the same year similar cars were started to Cashel and Thurles, and from Clonmel to Carrick and Waterford. In the first start there was a great advantage in obtaining a supply of capital

114

horses, intended for the army, and which were thrown on the market by the peace of 1815. They were bought at prices varying from ten to fifteen pounds. One of these horses drew a car with six passengers with ease at the rate of seven miles an hour. This was a wonderful improvement on the 'ould Irish jaunting car', with its miserable jade of a horse, which the town or village innkeeper let out, with its wild driver, at an exorbitant rate to the helpless traveller.

Encouraged by the success of his first conveyances, Mr Bianconi extended his establishment, opening lines in the most remote districts, as from Longford to Ballina and Belmullet, two hundred and one miles north-west from Dublin; from Athlone to Galway and Clifden, one hundred and eighty-three miles west from Dublin; from Limerick to Tralee and Cahirciveen, two hundred and thirty-three miles south-west from Dublin.

By this time the demand for first-class horses having diminished, the breeding of them ceased, and it was necessary to put two horses to the cars. The size of the cars was, however, enlarged, so as to hold four passengers instead of three on each side. Gradually the two-wheeled cars were displaced by four-wheeled cars, drawn by two, three or four horses, according to the traffic on the several roads.

In 1843, when Mr Bianconi made his first statement to the British Association at Cork, he had on his establishment a hundred vehicles, including mail coaches and cars of all sizes, capable of carrying from four to twenty passengers each, and travelling eight or nine miles an hour, at the low rate of a penny farthing a mile, going over three thousand eight hundred miles daily, and calling at one hundred and forty stations.

This success brought similar conveyances into the field in other parts of Ireland, and all over the country communication was easy and cheap, often cheaper than the journeys could have been made on foot, not to speak of the enormous saving of time. Fourteen years afterwards, when the second statement was laid before the British Association, the growth of railway communication had necessarily affected and diminished Mr Bianconi's establishment, but he still had sixty-seven conveyances in use, travelling daily four thousand two hundred and forty-four miles, and extending over portions of twenty-two counties, and requiring the use of above nine hundred horses.

Such in brief are the statistics of the establishment; now for some of the results, which I shall chiefly state in Mr Bianconi's own words. In the first place, as to the direct commercial and economical advantages, he says: 'I found, as communication between different localities was extended, the consumption of manufactured goods greatly increased. The competition of those availing themselves of the facilities of travelling was so great that, instead of buying from local retail shopkeepers after many profits, they were enabled to obtain the supplies nearer the manufacturer. In the remote parts of Ireland, for instance, on my opening the communication from Tralee to Cahirciveen in the south, Galway to Clifden in the west, and Ballina to Belmullet in the north-west, purchasers who had been obliged to give eight-pence or ninepence a yard for calico for shirts, subsequently paid only three-pence or fourpence, thus enabling that portion of the population who could previously badly afford only one shirt each, to have two for a less price than was paid for one; and at the same ratio other commodities came into general use at reduced prices. The resources of the country, many of which lay so long unproductive, were opened up. For instance, I enabled the fisher-men on the western coast to avail themselves of a rapid transit for their fresh fish, which being a very perishable article would be comparatively profitless unless its conveyance to Dublin and other suitable markets could be ensured within a given time. The amount realised by this valuable traffic is almost incredible, and has, in my opinion, largely contributed to the comfort and independence now so happily contrasting with the lamentable condition the west of Ireland presented a few years since.'

There was also direct encouragement given to agriculture as well as to trade. When there were one hundred and forty stations for the change of horses, the consumption of hay was from three to four thousand tons annually, and of oats from thirty to forty thousand barrels, all of which were purchased in their respective localities.

Each of these one hundred and forty stations had from one groom to six, and even eight; and there were about one hundred drivers for one thousand three hundred horses. The men were paid according to the line, the least pay being given to those on well-frequented lines, where there was more certainty of gratuities from travellers. They were promoted according to their services and conduct. Personal inspection was impossible in so extended an establish-ment, but the men were put on their good behaviour, and on the whole they were a well-conducted, trustworthy staff.

But while the tourists journeyed from town to town in Bianconi's uncomfortable cars, a fearful calamity impended over the country. In 1845 the potato crop showed extensive symptoms of disease and on 26 June *The Times* reported the condition of the people with accuracy in the following words: 'The facts of Irish destitution are ridiculously simple. They are almost too commonplace to be told. The people have not enough to eat. They are suffering a real, though artificial, famine.'

The Great Hunger had arrived.

BOOK TWO

The Great Famine and After

Is ní hé Dia cheap riamh an obair seo,
Daoine bochta do chur le fán,
Iad a chur sa phoorhouse go dubhach is glas orthu,
San lánamha leithscartha go bhfaighdís bás.
Na leanaí thógfaidís suas le macanais,
Sciobtaí uathu iad gan trua gan taise dhóibh.
Ar bheagán lóin ach soup na haindheise,
Gan máthair le freagairt dóibh dá bhfaighdís bás.

Nach trua san uaisle 'bhfuil morán cuid acu
Ag díol as an obair seo le Rí na nGrás;
Agus fearaibh bochta an tsaoil ná fuair riamh aon saidbhreas
Ach dian obair ó aois go bás.
Siad na prátaí dubha d'fhuig ár muintir scaipithe,
Do chuir sa phoorhouse iad, 's anonn thar farraige;
Is i reilig an tSléibhe tá na céadta díobh treascartha,
Agus Rí na bhflaitheas go réidh ár gcás.

No work of God's are these deeds accursed,
The poor dispersed in grief and pain,
The poorhouse gates that clanging close on them,
And wedlock bands for ever rent in twain.
The children they reared, with parents' care for them,
The poorhouse bare doth rudely tear from them.
Or should they die, no cry their mother hears,
Though they be lying near, by hunger slain.

Oh pity the proud ones, all earth possessing
That for these distresses must surely pay,
Oh, sad their fate, who the poor oppressing
Do richer grow by their moans each day.
The potatoes that failed, brought the nation to agony,
The poorhouse bare, and the dreadful coffin ship.
And in mountain graves do they in hundreds lie,
By hunger taken to their beds of clay.

WATERFORD FAMINE SONG

FAMINE AND EMIGRATION

A MILLION people died, either from famine or its attendant diseases, between 1845 and 1850. The revolutionary leader, John Mitchel, saw them:

BANDS OF EXTERMINATED peasants trooping to the already too full poorhouses; straggling columns of hunted wretches, with their old people, wives and little ones, wending their way to Cork or Waterford to take shipping for America; the people not yet ejected frightened and desponding, with no interest in the land they tilled, no property in the house above their heads, no food, no arms, with the slavish habits bred by long ages of oppression ground into their souls and that momentary proud flash of passionate hope, kindled by O'Connell's agitation, long since dimmed by bitter hunger and hardship.

William Bennett spent six weeks touring the country when the famine was at its worst. This is his account of Belmullet, county Mayo, written in March of the year the people afterwards called 'black 47':

WE NOW PROCEEDED to visit the district beyond the town within the Mullet. The cabins cluster the roadsides, and are scattered over the face of the bog, in the usual Irish manner, where the country is thickly inhabited. Several were pointed out as 'freeholders'; that is,

Bridget O'Donnell and her children, victims of the famine

such as had come wandering over the land, and 'squatted' down on any unoccupied spot, owning no fealty, and paying no rent. Their neighbours had probably built them the cabin in fourandtwenty hours; expecting the same service in turn for themselves should occasion require it—which a common necessity renders these poor people always willing to do for each other. Whatever little bit of ground they may reclaim around the cabin is necessarily done as much by stealth as possible; and the appearance of neglect and wretchedness is naturally carried out to the utmost; for should there be any visible improvement, down comes the landlord or his agent, with a demand for rent. The moral effect of such a state of things is obvious to the least reflecting mind. How far does its existence lie at the very basis of the low social condition of the people? I mention it here not as peculiar to this district. It is an element pervading large portions of Ireland; entering into the very growth of a population ever—by habit and education—on the verge of pauperism, and of whom the landlord, rarely coming near the property, knows little, and unfortunately in many instances cares less. The superior landlord—the nominal owner of a wide domain—has often very little interest, and no direct influence; or from encumbrances and limitations—perhaps ever since it came into his possession—he finds it a disagreeable and vexatious property, and dislikes it; or is really poor, and yet cannot relieve himself by reason of these difficulties. Here is society dislocated at *both ends*. Is Irish disorganization anything surprising? The natural influences and expenditure of property in creating artificial wants and means of livelihood, withdrawn from their own sources, and the people thrown back entirely upon the soil, with a bounty upon the veriest thriftlessness and least remove above the lowest animal conditions of life! Under such a state of things—not the accident of today, but the steady and regular growth of years and a system— a population is nurtured, treading constantly on the borders of starvation; checked only by a crisis like the present, to which it inevitably leads, and almost verifying the worst Malthusian doctrines.

Many of the cabins were holes in the bog, covered with a layer of turves, and not distinguishable as human habitations from the surrounding moor, until close down upon them. The bare sod was about the best material of which any of them were constructed. Doorways, not doors, were usually provided at both sides of the bettermost—back and front—to take advantage of the way of the wind. Windows and chimneys, I think, had no existence.

A second apartment or division of any kind within was exceedingly rare. Furniture, properly so called, I believe may be stated at *nil*. I would not speak with certainty, and wish not to with exaggeration—we were too much overcome to note specifically—but as far as memory serves, we saw neither bed, chair, nor table, at all. A chest, a few iron or earthen vessels, a stool or two, the dirty rags and night-coverings, formed about the sum total of the best furnished. Outside many were all but unapproachable, from the mud and filth surrounding them; the same inside, or worse if possible, from the added closeness, darkness, and smoke. We spent the whole morning in visiting these hovels indiscriminately, or swayed by the representations and entreaties of the dense retinue of wretched creatures, continually augmenting, which gathered round, and followed us from place to place—avoiding only such as were known to be badly infected with fever, which was sometimes sufficiently perceptible from without, by the almost intolerable stench. And now language utterly fails me in attempting to depict the state of the wretched inmates. I would not willingly add another to the harrowing details that have been told; but still they are the facts of actual experience, for the knowledge of which we stand accountable. I have certainly sought out one of the most remote and destitute corners; but still it is within the bounds of our Christian land, under our Christian government, and entailing upon us—both as individuals and as members of a human community—a Christian responsibility from which no one of us can escape. My hand trembles while I write. The scenes of human misery and degradation we witnessed still haunt my imagination, with the vividness and power of some horrid and tyranous delusion, rather than the features of a sober reality. We entered a cabin. Stretched in one dark corner, scarcely visible, from the smoke and rags that covered them, were three children huddled together, lying there *because they were too weak to rise*, pale and ghastly, their little limbs—on removing a portion of the filthy covering—perfectly emaciated, eyes sunk, voice gone, and evidently in the last stage of actual starvation. Crouched over the turf embers was another form, wild and all but naked, scarcely human in appearance. It stirred not nor noticed us. On some straw, soddened upon the ground, moaning piteously, was a shrivelled old woman, imploring us to give her something— baring her limbs partly, to show how the skin hung loose from the bones, as soon as she attracted our attention. Above her, on something like a ledge, was a young woman, with sunken cheeks—a mother I have no doubt—who

124

scarcely raised her eyes in answer to our enquiries, but pressed her hand upon her forehead, with a look of unutterable anguish and despair. Many cases were widows, whose husbands had recently been taken off by the fever, and thus their only pittance, obtained from the public works, entirely cut off. In many the husbands or sons were prostrate, under that horrid disease—the results of long-continued famine and low living—in which first the limbs, and then the body, swell most frightfully, and finally burst. We entered upwards of fifty of these tenements. The scene was one and invariable, differing in little but the number of the sufferers, or of the groups, occupying the several corners within. The whole number was often not to be distinguished, until—the eye having adapted itself to the darkness—they were pointed out, or were heard, or some filthy bundle of rags and straw was perceived to move. Perhaps the poor children presented the most piteous and heart-rending spectacle. Many were too weak to stand, their little limbs attenuated—except where the frightful swellings had taken the place of

A famine meal

A scene at the gate of a workhouse during the famine

previous emaciation—beyond the power of volition when moved. Every infantile expression entirely departed; and in some, reason and intelligence had evidently flown. Many were remnants of families, crowded together in one cabin; orphaned little relatives taken in by the equally destitute, and even strangers, for these poor people are kind to one another to the end. In one cabin was a sister, just dying, lying by the side of her little brother, just dead. I have worse than this to relate, but it is useless to multiply details, and they are, in fact, unfit. They did but rarely complain. When inquired of, what was the matter, the answer was alike in all—*tha shein ukrosh*—indeed the hunger. We truly learned the terrible meaning of that sad word *ukrosh*. There were many touching incidents. We should have gone on, but the pitiless storm had now arisen, beating us back with a force and violence against which it was difficult to stand; and a cutting rain, that drove us for shelter beneath a

126

bank, fell on the crowd of poor creatures who continued to follow us un-mitigatedly. My friend the clergyman had distributed the tickets for meal to the extent he thought prudent; and he assured me wherever we went it would be a repetition of the same all over the country, and even worse in the far off mountain districts, as this was near the town, where some relief could reach. It was my full impression that one-fourth of those we saw were in a dying state, beyond the reach of any relief that could now be afforded; and many more would follow. The lines of this day can never be effaced from my memory. These were our fellow-creatures, children of the same parent, born with our common feelings and affections,with an equal right to live as any one of us, with the same purposes of existence, the same spiritual and immortal natures, the same work to be done, the same judgement seat to be summoned to, and the same eternal goal.

Parts of west Cork and Kerry were particularly badly hit by the famine. Bennett wrote about conditions in and around the town of Kenmare:

KILLARNEY, KENMARE, Glengarriff, are names which have long been associated with all that is lovely and beautiful in the Sister Isle. The first-named I had visited on a former occasion; the two latter were new ground to me, but an investigation of the scenery was not now the object.

It was late in the evening when we arrived at Kenmare, tired and a good deal exhausted. I had looked upon our painful mission as now completed, not having any idea of the awfully wretched condition of this town and neighbourhood, until accounts had begun to reach us, the last day or two, on approaching its vicinity. We were beset immediately with the most terrific details of the want and sufferings of the people: indeed it could not be concealed. The sounds of woe and wailing resounded in the streets throughout the night. I felt extremely ill, and was almost overcome.

In the morning I was credibly informed that nine deaths had taken place during the night in the open streets, from sheer want and exhaustion. The poor people came in from the rural districts in such numbers, in the hopes of getting some relief, that it was utterly impossible to meet their most urgent

Carrying out the dead during the famine

exigencies, and therefore they came in literally to die; and I might see several families lying about in the open streets, actually dying of starvation and fever, within a stone's throw of the inn. I went out accordingly. In the corner of an old enclosure, to which my steps were directed, on the bare ground, under the open heaven was a remnant of three. One had just been carted away who had died in the night; the father had died before; the rest could not long survive. A little further, in a cask, placed like a dog-kennel, was a poor boy, who had lain there some time, in high fever, without friends or relatives. I proceeded down the main street. In the middle of it, on a little straw, under an open erection, made by placing two uprights and a board across them, were two women, horrible to behold, in the last stages of consumptive fever, brought on by evident starvation. The town itself is overwhelmed with poverty; and the swollen limbs, emaciated countenances, and other hideous forms of disease to be seen about, were innumerable. In no other part of Ireland had I seen people falling on their knees to beg. It was difficult to sit over breakfast after this . . .

The want of clothing is as great as the want of food. The wan, aged and sunken countenances, and the silent beseeching look, without a word spoken, of some of the women and girls, is what enters into the heart deepest, and is the most difficult to bear. To describe properly the state of things in some of these wretched districts, is a vain attempt. It is impossible—it is inconceivable. Starvation—a word that has now become so familiar, as scarcely to awaken a painful idea—is *not* being two or three days deficient of food. It is something quite different; and the effects of dwindling and insufficient nourishment upon a whole population, upon the mass of men, women and the little children; the disease, the emaciation, the despair, the extinction of everything human beyond it, are utterly past the powers of description, or even of imagination, without witnessing. I am in possession of details beyond anything that has appeared in print, or, I believe, in private circulation; in fact, for the sake of poor humanity, unfit to communicate. My mind was at times so struck down, that for days together the pen has refused its office; the appalling spectacles have seemed to float between, whenever I attempted it, and to paralyse every effort. The loss of a parent, of a child, we know what it is in any one of our families. If the causes are, or appear to have been, in any way within the reach of neglected assistance, or of human control, we know how manifold the agony is increased. Multiply this into all the cabins, the populous way-sides, the far-off solitary mountain hamlets, vivify the details of famine and pestilence, by thousands and tens of thousands, throughout the length and breadth of Ireland, and we may have some idea of the voice of anguish and lamentation that now ascends from her whole land.

The anguish continued for many years. In his book *Life and Death in Ireland as witnessed in 1849*, Spenser T. Hall, editor of *The Sherwood Magazine*, described the condition of the people in the vicinity of Limerick city:

INTO ONE OF their cabins it was that now for the first time I entered. It was a poor one, yet (though almost without furniture) by no means one of the worst class. Still the sight of it pained me then. Its tenant was a widow, who a day or two before had surprised the chieftain by falling down and kissing his feet, as a welcome, on his and his lady's return after many years' absence in England! It is not irrational to suppose that there were more motives than one for that proceeding; and the result was what she probably anticipated—an occasional remembrance in

Distributing relief tickets in the turf market at Westport

coin, or scraps of food from the kitchen, near to which might every day be seen loitering a crowd of living skeletons, consisting mostly of *outsiders*; for many of the poor on this estate had regular employment, and very few of them were totally without it.

Ascending the mountain through such a profusion of verdure as I had never observed in England so early in the year—among underwood composed principally of the greatest and brightest hollies—we at length arrived at the boundary of the estate, and I was now made fully sensible of the meaning of the term *outsider*. Whilst the chieftain and the bailiff were taking shelter by the woodside, I thought I would go for a draught of water to a cabin at a short distance. The door to it was not much higher than that to many a common English pig-stye. Its window was a mere loop-hole and had never known the luxury of glass; and the floor I scarcely need say was without a pavement. The first salutation I had on entering was from the still animated skeleton of a dog, famished until it was hardly able to raise a bark; the second was a feeble female voice from a place within, that might fitly have served for the dog's kennel, but which was used as a sleeping room. By the little light struggling into the outer apartment I was just able to discern that an old table, on which stood a broken jug, composed the whole of its furniture. Into the inner room (or hole) no light penetrated; but in accents that betokened sad suffering its inmate told me that she was very ill, and I approached her as well as I could, being guided solely by her voice. When she found that I was a stranger she gave a faint shriek of terror, but was soon pacified by kindly words. She complained of getting rapidly worse and of being near her end, and said that those to whom she belonged were compelled, for the sake of trying to obtain food, thus to leave her alone. I asked if any doctor had been to see her. Such words seemed to have for her but an idle meaning, and she answered to the contrary in a tone of despair. Had no clergyman been near her? 'He hadn't then.' Had not a gentleman who was staying at ———House? 'No, they were *outside* to ———.' Who then did they belong to? 'Lord ——— ———.' Whatever was her complaint, I could only infer from her own description that the cause of it was destitution. Whether she were young or old I did not know; for as to *seeing* her, that was out of the question. But I did

Victims of the famine

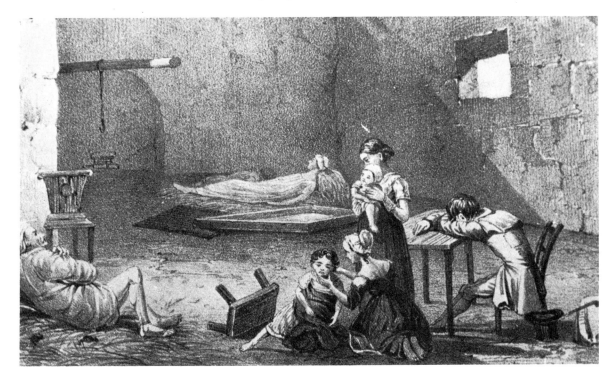

feel her poor bony hand as it received from mine the little coin I had to bestow towards buying some relief when her companions should return. Oh! I thought it was a young hand, but anyway it was that of death; and when next I went up to learn what more had been or could be done, the silence of death was there too; his work was finished and the place deserted! This then was starvation, and within sight of Limerick city, where hay at the time was selling at less than twenty shillings a ton! Hundreds of cattle were probably exported that week from Dublin and Cork to England. At all events, I myself saw, a few days afterwards, within a mile and a half of the very scene described, a cow in calf sold for forty-eight shillings, to enable a poor man, as he said, to pay his rent, which cow would have fetched in any English market, five or six pounds—perhaps more! Surely, thought I, the sun never before shone upon such a strange anomaly! Scenes like these and worse, soon became common to me, however, as the sequel will show; and from that hour (though the climate is a marvellous stimulant to the appetite) I never ate a good meal in Ireland without the heart-ache.

The country was leaderless by the time Spencer T. Hall reached Ireland. O'Connell was dead; so was Thomas Davis, the thinker and teacher who had tried in his newspaper, *The Nation*, to create a feeling of nationality among all the people, rich and poor, Catholic and Protestant. Davis's successor as editor of *The Nation*, the Ulster Protestant John Mitchel, exhorted the people during the famine years to pay no rent and to prevent by force the exportation of food from the country. He was arrested and transported. His colleagues, Smith O'Brien, John Dillon and Thomas F. Meagher tried to set off a rising in Munster but their effort failed. The simple fact was that the people were too weak to fight. The leaders of this '48 revolt got their share of abuse from various travellers. Randall M'Collum, in a book entitled *Sketches from the Highlands of Cavan taken during the Irish Famine*, said:

AN INCURABLE obstinacy and dogged selfishness seemed, like a demon, to have taken possession of these Young Irelanders; and with all his address, O'Connell could not keep within the bounds of law these patriots, who were set on self-immolation. It was a pity

132

that Mitchel was deprived the honour of a traitor's end. But the humanity of a Christian people interposed; and an act of mercy shown to those infatuated men has told for good on Smith O'Brien, who will, we trust, be soon restored to his quiet home, a wiser and a better man. For Mitchel there is no hope. His maladies are incurable, and as he is unfit for liberty, it is unsafe to have him at large. The Americans should look after him, and secure him in some asylum, ere he raise an insurrection among the slaves . . .

Another evil that these leaders have left behind, is the widespread disaffection that prevails among the Roman Catholic peasantry. It is notorious that, during the exciting news that was coming from the Crimea, in the course of the late war, every new difficulty and reverse that took place among the British forces, was caught up with avidity, and circulated among the peasantry, who made no secret of their delight at hearing of the disasters of the British army.

Dr Samuel Reynolds Hole, Dean of Rochester, visited Ireland in the fifties, and in a Galway hotel he met a waiter who gave him a first-hand account of the famine:

AH, BUT WE felt almost ashamed of being so full and comfortable, when our conversational attendant began to talk to us about the Great Famine. 'That's right, good gintlemen,' he said, 'niver forget, when ye've had your males, to thank the Lord as sends them. May ye niver know what it is to crave for food, and may ye niver see what I have seen, here in the town o' Galway. I mind the time when I lived yonder' (and he pointed to Kilroy's Hotel), 'and the poor craturs come crawling in from the country with their faces swollen, and grane, and yaller, along of the arbs they'd been atin'. We gave them bits and scraps, good gintlemen, and did what we could (the Lord be praised!), but they was mostly gone too far out o' life to want more than the priest and pity. I've gone out of a morning, gintlemen,' (his lip quivered as he spoke), 'and seen them lying dead in the square, with the green grass in their mouths.' And he turned away, (God bless his kind heart!), to hide the tears which did him so much honour.

Can history or imagination suggest a scene more awfully impressive than that which Ireland presented in the times of the Great Famine? The

Distributing clothing at Kilrush, 1849

sorrows of that visitation have been recorded by eloquent, earnest men; but they come home to us with a new and startling influence when we hear of them upon Irish ground. Most vividly can we realise the wreck when he, who hardly swam ashore and escaped, points to the scene of peril; and while the storm-clouds still drift in the far horizon, and the broken timbers float upon the seething wave, describes, with an exactness horrible to himself, that last amazement and despair.

In the beautiful land of the merry-hearted, 'all joy was darkened, the mirth of the land was gone'. In the country of song, and dance, and laughter, there was not heard, wherever that famine came, one note of music, nor one cheerful sound, only the gasp of dying men, and the mourners' melancholy wail. The green grass of the Emerald Isle grew over a nation's grave. The crowning plague of Egypt was transcended here, for not only in some districts was there in every house 'one dead', but there were homes in which there was but one living—homes, in which one little child was found, calling upon father, mother, brothers and sisters, to wake from their last, long sleep, homes from which the last survivor fled away, in wild alarm, from those whom living he had loved so well. Fathers were seen vainly endeavouring (such was their weakness) to dig a grave for their children, reeling and staggering with the useless spade in their hands. The poor widow, who had left her home to beg a coffin for her last, lost child, fell beneath her burden upon the road and died. The mendicant had now no power to beg. The drivers of the public cars went into cottages, and found *all* dead, or Rachel weeping for her children, and praying that die she might. By the seaside, men seeking shell-fish, fell down upon the sands, and, impotent to rise, were drowned. First they began to bury corpses, coffinless, then they could not bury them at all. Of indignities and mutilations, when then befell, I will not, for I cannot, speak.

Indeed, it may be asked, wherefore should we repeat at all, these sad, heart-rending details? Because, the oftener they are had in painful remembrance, the less likely they are to recur in terrible reality; because

> *Never did any public misery*
> *Rise of itself; God's plagues still grounded are*
> *On common stains of our humanity;*
> *And to the flame which ruineth mankind*
> *Man gives the matter, or at least the wind.*

The fortunate ones reached America in the coffin-ships, many with the aid of landlords anxious to clear their estates through the financial assistance of the government. Harriet Martineau, a friend of Wordsworth and Coleridge, on her way through the town of Castlebar, county Mayo, witnessed the departure of a family to Boston. Her account of Ireland was published in the *Daily News* and reprinted in 1852 in book form under the title *Letters from Ireland*. She wrote:

Evicted, a scene in Galway, 1847

THE POPULATION OF Castlebar was, if we were correctly informed, six thousand before the Famine; and it is now between three and four thousand. Many have gone to the grave; but more have removed to other countries. Large sums are arriving by post to carry away many more. We were yesterday travelling by the public car, when, at a distance of a few miles from Castlebar, on approaching a cluster of houses, we were startled—to say the truth, our blood ran cold—at the loud cry of a young girl who ran across the road, with a petticoat over her head, which did not conceal the tears on her convulsed face. A crowd of poor people came

136

from—we know not where—most of them in tears, some weeping quietly, others with unbearable cries. A man, his wife and three young children were going to America. They were well dressed, all shod, and the little girls bonneted. There was some delay—much delay—about where to put their great box; and the delay was truly painful. Of all the crowd, no-one cast a momentary glance at anybody but the departing emigrants. The inquisitiveness, the vigilance, the begging, characteristic of those who surround cars, were all absent. All eyes were fixed on the neighbours who were going away for ever. The last embraces were terrible to see; but worse were the kissings and the claspings of hands during the long minutes that remained after the woman and children had taken their seats . . . There it was, the pain and the passion: and the shrill united cry, when the car moved on, rings in our ears, and long will ring when we hear of emigration. They threw up their arms and

Getting a clean bill of health before emigrating

wailed. When a distant turn in the road showed the hamlet again, we could just distinguish the people standing where we left them. As for the family, we could not see the man, who was on the other side of the car. The woman's face was soon like other people's, and the children were eating oatcake very composedly.

Those who survived the famine and the disease and the journey to America in the coffin-ships sent money home to help their relatives escape from the doomed island. The following letter was written by a girl whose passage was paid to New York from Kingwilliamstown, county Cork, by the crown estates:

Michael Boyan Esqre.
Kingwilliamstown Kanturk Post Office
County of Cork, Ireland
to be forwarded to Mr Alexander MCarthy, of same place.

New York September 22nd, 1850.

My Dr. Father and Mother Brothers and Sisters,
I write these few lines to you hopeing That these few lines may find you all in as good State of health as I am at present thank God I received your welcome letter To me Dated 22nd. of May which was A Credit to me for the Stile and Elligence of its Fluent Language but I must Say Rather Flattering My Dr. Father I must only say that this is a good place and A good Country for if one place does not Suit A man he can go to Another and can very easy please himself But there is one thing thats Ruining this place Especially the Frontirs towns and Cities where the Flow of Emmigration is most the Emmigrants has not money enough to Take them to the Interior of the Country which oblidges them to Remain here in New York and the like places for which Reason Causes the less demand for Labour and also the great Reduction in wages for this Reason I would advise no one to Come to America that would not have Some Money after landing here that (would) Enable them to go west in case they would get no work to do here but any

138

man or woman without a family are fools that would not venture and Come to this plentyful Country where no man or woman ever Hungerd or ever will and where you will not be Seen Naked, but I can asure you there are Dangers upon Dangers Attending Comeing here but my Friends nothing Venture nothing have Fortune will favour the brave have Courage and prepare yourself for the next time that, that worthy man Mr. Boyen is Sending out the next lot, and Come you all Together Couragiously and bid adieu to that lovely place the land of our Birth. that place where the young and old joined Together in one Common Union, both night and day Engaged in Innocent Amusement, But alas. I am now Told its the Gulf of Misersry oppression Degradetion and Ruin of evry Discription which I am Sorry to hear of so Doleful a History to Be told of our Dr. Country This my Dr. Father induces me to Remit to you in this Letter 20 Dollars that is four Pounds thinking it might be Some Acquisition to you untill you might Be Clearing away from that place all together and the Sooner the Better for Beleive me I could not Express how great would be my joy at seeing you all here Together where you would never want or be at a loss for a good Breakfast and Dinner. So prepare as soon as possible for this will be my last Remittince untill I see you all here. Bring with you as much Tools as you can as it will cost you nothing to Bring them And as for your Clothing you need not care much But that I would like that yourself would Bring one good Shoot of Cloth that you would spare until you come here And as for Mary She need not mind much as I will have for her A Silk Dress A Bonnet and Viel according and Ellen I need not mention what I will have for her I can fit her well you are to Bring Enough Flannels and do not form it at home as the way the weay Flannel at home and here is quite different for which reason I would Rather that you would not form any of it untill you Come, with the Exception of whatever Quantity of Drawers you have you can make them at ahome But make them Roomly Enough But Make No Jackets.

My Dr. Father I am Still in the Same place but do not Intend to Stop here for the winter. I mean to come into New York and there Spend the winter Thade Houlehan wrote to me Saying that if I wished to go up the Country that he would send me money but I declined so doing untill you Come and then after you Coming if you think it may be Better for us to Remain here or go west it will be for you to judge but untill then I will Remain here. Dan Keliher Tells me that you Knew more of the House

Emigrants at Cork Quay

Carpentery than he did himself and he can earn from twelve to fourteen Shilling a day that is seven Shilling British and he also Tells me that Florence will do very well and that Michl can get a place Right off as you will not be In the Second day when you can Bind him to any Trade you wish And as for John he will Be Very Shortly Able to Be Bound two So that I have Every Reason to Believe that we will all do will Together So as that I am sure its not for Slavery I want you to Come here no its for affording My Brothers and Sisters And I an oppertunity of Showing our Kindness and Gratitude and Comeing on your Seniour days that we would be placed in that possision that you my Dr. Father and Mother could walk about Lesuirly and Indepenly without Requireing your Labour an object which I am Sure will not fail even by Myself if I was oblidged to do it without the assistance of Brother or Sister for my Dr. Father and Mother.

I am proud and happy to Be away from where the County Charges man or the poor Rates man or any other Rates man would have the Satisfaction of once Inpounding my cow or any other article of mine Oh how happy I feel and am sure to have look as The Lord had not it destined for me to get married to Some Loammun or another at home that after a few months he and I may be an Incumberance upon you or perhaps in the poor house by

140

this, So my Dr. Father according as I had Stated to you I hope that whilst you are at home I hope that you will give my Sister Mary that privelage of Injoying herself Innocently on any occation that She pleases so far as I have said Innocently and as for my Dr. Ellen I am in Raptures of joy when I think of one day Seeing her and you all at the dock in New York and if I do not have a good Bottle of Brandy for you Awaiting your arrival its a Causion.

Well I have only to tell my Dr. Mother to Bring all her bed Close and also to bring the Kittle and an oven and have handles to them and do not forget the Smoothing Irons and Beware when you are on board to Bring some good floor and Ingage with the Captain Cook and he will do it Better for you for very little and also Bring some whiskey and give them the Cook and some Sailors that you may think would do you any good to give them a Glass once in a time and it may be no harm.

And Dr. Father when you are Comeing here if you Possiblely can Bring My Uncle Con I would Be glad that you would and I am sure he would be of the greatest acquisision to you on board and also Tell Mary Keeffe that if her Child died that I will pay her passage very Shortly and when you are Comeing do not be frightened Take Courage and be Determined and bold in your Undertaking as the first two or three days will be the worst to you and mind whatever happens on board Keep your own temper and do not speak angry to any or hasty the Mildest Man has the best chance on board So you make your way with evey one and further you are to speak

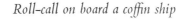

Roll-call on board a coffin ship

to Mr Boyan and he I am sure will get one Request for you Mr Boyan will do it for me, when you are to Come ask Mr Boyan to give you a few lines to the Agent or Berth Master of the Ship that will Secure to you the Second Cabin which I am sure Mr Boyan will do and as soon as you Receive this letter write to me and let me know about every thing when you are to come and what time and state Particulars of evry thing to me and Direct as before. And if you are to come Shortly when you come to Liberpool wright to me also and let me know when you are to sail and the name of the Ship you sail in as I will be uneasy untill I get an answer.

No more at present But that you will give Mr and Mrs Boyan my best love and respect And let me know how they and family are as they would or will not Be ever Better than I would wish them to be also Mrs Milton and Charles Mr and Mrs Roche and family Mr and Mrs day and family Mr Walsh and as for his family I am sure are all well Mr and Mrs Sullivan and family Mrs O Brien Con Sheehan wife and family all the Hearlihys and familys Tim Leahy and family own Sullivan of Cariganes and family Darby Guinee and family John Calleghan and family Timoth Calleghan and family Timothy Sheehan and Mother So no more at present form your Ever Dear and Loveing Child.
Margaret MCarthy.

In 1841 the population of Ireland was eight million one hundred and seventy-five thousand and would probably have reached eight and a half million by 1851, had the blight not struck; in fact, the population that year was six and a half million. By the century's end emigration had further reduced it to about four million.

THE PRIEST AND THE
LANDLORD

IN THE years following the great famine the number of travellers who left us an account of Ireland in book form decreased. The Grand Tour of Europe, with an excursion through Ireland at its end, went out of fashion in the 'thirties, and from the beginning of the 'fifties onwards those who came to Ireland were, it would appear, much more interested in giving their impressions of the increasingly complex political scene than in commenting on living conditions or on the changes in Irish society.

Harriet Martineau, having seen the condition of the country in the wake of the great hunger, thought that the most striking new features of Irish life, apart from emigration, were the movements of 'the two great background figures', the landlord and the priest. She realised that the famine had shocked the priests into taking a greater interest in the political scene and while she was alarmed by the growing animus between them and the landlords, her greatest fear was that any sign of arrogance on the part of the clergy might be an encouragement to the people to use violence in their attempts to redress agrarian wrongs. She had come to the conclusion that in the west at any rate a lot of ill-feeling towards the landlords was in connection with Protestant proselytism, and she felt that the ill-feeling would increase 'if the Protestant zealots go on doing as some of them are doing now'. As for the relationship between priest and landlord, she wrote on October 5, 1852:

AS WEEK AFTER week passes away, and we travel from moorland to village, and from coast to city, the old state of

Consulting the priest, Claremorris, county Mayo 1887

Ireland comes out to the eye more clearly from the new innovations put upon it; and the innovations themselves become more distinct in their operation as the old state of things reveals itself to the vigilant observer. At first, there is a confusion, as in a dissolving view, when a new scene presents itself before another is gone; but, by degrees, the two separate themselves into a background and a foreground, and are equally clear in their respective distances. Day by day now we watch with more interest the movements of the two great background figures—the landlord and the priest—observing how they are themselves watching each other, and the innovations proceeding before their eyes. This jealous watchfulness is the only thing in which they agree—unless, indeed, it be in their both being very unhappy.

Very unhappy they both are. The landlord has for centuries been a sort of prince on his own territory. His lands spread along the sea and over the mountains, and include the rivers, like a royal dominion. A man who calls mountains and rivers his own cannot but feel himself a prince; and princely is the pride of the Irish landlord. His word has been law, and there has been no-one to call him to account till within a quarter of a century. First, his old enemy, the priest, was emancipated; and now, one attack upon his prerogative after another has driven him to desperation. He believes himself the object of legislative persecution—he is called to account about the letting of his lands— he is rated for the support of his poor—his solvent tenants throw up their farms and leave the country—and he is not allowed to evict in his own way those who cannot pay rent. His rents fail him; and, when he cannot pay his debts, his estates are sold for the benefit of his creditors; and he finds himself stripped of lands, power and position, with little (perhaps too little) solace of sympathy and indulgent construction. Those who have sunk are, for the most part, quiet—as beseems their dignity. Those who are sinking, or in fear of sinking, are very far from being quiet. They scold and vituperate the priest, as if both were in rivalship about rising, instead of being both under the same doom of fall. There is nothing more painful than landlord language about the priests; unless it be the ever-strengthening suspicion in the observer's mind of the part borne by the priests in the destruction of the landlord.

The priest is as far from peace and prosperity as his great rival. He is in deep poverty, from the depopulation of the rural districts, which were his bank up to the time of the famine. He is reduced to follow the Protestant zealots from house to house, and set up his sacerdotal threats against the promises and praises of the emissaries who are seducing his flock from him. He is confused with rustics who hold up their Bibles before his eyes; and little children are lifted up in his path to spit Scripture texts in his face. He is not allowed to manage his duty in his own way, and to take care of his own position. It is clearly understood, among both his friends and his enemies, that he is controlled 'from headquarters', so that he is compelled to do what he knows to be rash, and forbidden to do what he believes to be best. About the Ribbon Societies, those may speak who have knowledge. We have none

145

beyond that which is possessed by all the world—that the priests know all about them, and that the priesthood have unbounded power over them. Whether it is true, as many believe, that the matter is managed by an authority above that of the resident priesthood—whether the resident priests are willing or unwilling participants in a system of secret and bloody conspiracy, is a matter of which we know nothing. All we can say is, that there can be no conspiracy against the property and life of the landlords that the priests are not fully informed of. Which is the more unhappy class of the two, there is no need to estimate. The landlord struggles, protests, or silently mourns, and sinks. The priest goes about with an unpleasant countenance—significant, discontented, suspicious; in his unreserved moments confiding to a friendly ear his regrets that Irish affairs are misunderstood 'at headquarters', that he is compelled to obey orders which he thinks ignorant and rash, and that the Wiseman movement was prematurely made; and while he thus unburdens his mind, he is sinking perhaps as fast as his rival.

The most remarkable figure among the Irish Catholic hierarchy was old John MacHale, Archbishop of Tuam. He had been the first bishop to come out strongly in favour of O'Connell's repeal programme; he had fought a long and bitter struggle against the national schools board, because he considered these schools a threat to Irish nationality. With less logic he opposed the entry of Catholic students into the new Queen's Colleges, arguing that history, logic, metaphysics, moral philosophy, geology and anatomy could not be studied under Protestant professors 'without exposing faith and morals to imminent danger'. Always his own man, he opposed the proclamation of the doctrine of papal infallibility at the Vatican Council in 1869–70. Mrs Houstun, one of the Protestant zealots referred to by Harriet Martineau, left us a description of an encounter with Dr MacHale in her book *Twenty Years in the Wild West*. She had opened a school in Mayo and was visited by the old Archbishop.

ON ONE EXCEPTIONALLY fine day in August, I, being then in the small exotic fernery, which in imagination carried me many a mile from chilly Ireland, was suddenly informed that two open carriages, both as full as they could hold of 'travellers', were about to turn

146

'round the rock' on the road that led to Delphi. In a moment, being alone in the house, I brought a field-glass to bear upon the enemy, and discovered that a 'cloud', not of 'majors', but of priests was darkening the horizon! That they had gone to 'inspect' the school did not for a moment enter my head, and yet, *que diable allaient ils faire dans cette galère?*

Possibly, though not probably, those eight black-coated men (for eight I had ascertained there were), had been seized with a desire to see 'the mountains', and were out on a *shockarawn* accordingly; or they might—seeing that the only burial ground in this mountain district was in the most dilapidated and disgraceful condition—have taken it into their reverend heads to inspect the place, and to make arrangements for the more decent interment of the bodies of the faithful.

Whether or not to either of these causes could be attributed the length of time which elapsed before I again caught sight (at the turn of the very sharp rocky angle that shuts out any further view of the public pathway) of the

Parish priest's visit to Dooagh, Achill Island

An eviction in county Kerry

horses' heads matters little. One fact is certain, namely, that the idea of *my* receiving a visit from these mysterious gentry never for a moment occurred to me. Judge then of my surprise, when—having by that time almost given up thinking about them—a 'boy' ran up breathlessly from the stables with the information that the Archbishop of 'Tume' and 'all the clairgy' were driving up to the house! This was indeed a surprise; and as from the drawing-room window I watched the descent, in the first place, of a stalwart priest, and then, resting a hand on his arm, that of a very old, but still erect and apparently healthy old man, the wish that it had not befallen upon me (in my unprotected state) to receive this extremely unwelcome party was very strong within me. There was, however, no help for it, and nothing remained

148

but to receive my visitors courteously, and wait for an explanation of the visit.

After shaking hands with 'John of Tuam', regarding whom I had of course heard much, and exchanging bows with the remainder of the confraternity who, as it appeared to me, stood in great awe of their vigorous ruler, the latter took upon himself to explain the reason of his coming so far (he had never, he said, visited this portion of his diocese before) into the mountains.

'We have known for some time past', he said, 'that there is a mission school, as it is called, in this neighbourhood; but I delayed, till I could take the journey, doing anything about it. We have been into the school-house now, and made sure of its being true (as I was informed) that there are no emblems in the place.'

'Emblems, your Grace!' I put in (for I addressed him according to his legitimate clerical rank, though he did speak with a brogue, and was not *quite* the cleanest old man with whom I had ever come in contact). 'Emblems', I repeated. 'I beg your pardon, but my ignorance in such matters must be my excuse. The room, too, in which your Grace has been is private property, and, although had you asked for it, I should willingly have given you permission to . . .'

But I was not allowed to proceed. John of Tuam had clearly not bearded the Pope of Rome on his throne, to be 'put down' in her own small drawing-room, by a woman. With a wave of his hand, at which his satellites looked high approval, he proceeded to say that until 'emblems' were applied to the walls of the school-house he could not permit it to exist. Emblems were with 'the Church' a *sine qua non,* and emblems the old Archbishop declared that he would have.

Oh! how at the authoritative words the free British blood within me boiled and stirred! By what right, I longed to ask him (only he was so old that I refrained), could he close a school which was built on another man's land, and over which he could claim no *earthly* power? The truth was that, being of an autocratic nature and in the habit of saying that his will—namely, that of 'the Church'—was 'law', he, in a senile kind of fashion, went a step too far. Close the school of course he could not, but the power was undoubtedly his to prevent any Roman Catholic child from entering it, and this power he clearly intended to exercise. A priest has only to threaten the parents with

149

refusal to, in their last moments, 'anoint' them, and, ardently as they desire to have their children rescued from ignorance, not one amongst them would, I venture to say, brave the fearful menace which is, in the hands of the priesthood, a weapon of such tremendous force.

After a short while the old man and I understood each other. I explained to him how carefully I had guarded the children of the Romish faith from any interference with their religion. 'But', I said, '*we* Protestants have also our prejudices, and our points of belief. In the Delphi school there are nearly as many Protestants as there are Catholic children, and I greatly doubt whether any one of the Scotchmen would, in the event of your Grace's *request*' (and I laid a marked stress upon the word) 'being complied with, allow their little ones to come to school. Strive as I may, I have never been able to make them understand that you Catholics are not worshippers of wood and stone and painted canvas; and therefore the poor things would see in the emblems of which you make so great a point, simply the idols to which you are accused of addressing your prayers.'

It is needless to relate the conversation, one of no long duration, which ensued. It ended (after my visitors had been offered refreshment, and had refused to partake of our bread and salt) in my informing the Archbishop that I possessed no power whatever in the matter of which he had been speaking. I would, I told him, consult 'the Captain', and also the Protestant parents, as to the advisability of placing crucifixes, pictures of the Blessed Virgin, etc., etc., upon the interior walls of the school-house. Eventually I would, I said, inform him of the result.

'It was chiefly for the Scotch and English that the affair was set on foot', I concluded by saying, 'and if they object to their admission I will not be the one to force upon their children's notice that which is repugnant to their own feelings.'

'Then I have your promise?' the old man said unctuously, as he held my hand at parting.

'My promise that I will do my best, without giving offence to others, to afford those poor little ignorant waifs and strays, whose parents are so earnestly craving for it, the blessings of education. We cannot in any way coerce in this matter our Protestant *employés*. The decision is one for their own consciences alone to make, and we should consider ourselves as guilty of wrong-doing were we to interfere with them; whilst, on the other hand, we should undoubtedly be equally blamable if we paid no respect to the feelings and convictions of the Catholics who depend for their daily bread upon our retaining them on the land.'

These were amongst the last words which passed between me and this undoubtedly remarkable man—this most pugnacious of the Church Militant's western champions. I had given him a hint—but only a hint, for, in truth, I felt thoroughly ashamed of the efforts which had been made by zealous proselytisers to induce us to force our papistical people, on pain of eviction, to attend our churches, and otherwise demean themselves as converts, I had given the redoubtable 'John of *Tume*', then, a hint that, 'an we would, we could' use engines calculated still further to depopulate the country, and possibly, though not probably, secure to the heretics a 'joomper' or two from their forefathers' faith; but, instead of being aroused by the mild suggestion, he clearly considered the semi-threat too puerile to be noticed. Escorted, as on his arrival, by his *aides*, the old man went his way, an obstinate resolve to hold his own being clearly visible on every line of his strongly-marked countenance.

It is, perhaps, scarcely necessary to say that, after this domiciliary visit, not a single Roman Catholic child ever set its foot again in Delphi school.

In places evictions were carried out on a most extensive scale. In the west of Ireland, particularly in Mayo, there was a mania to form large grazing farms, in the hope of constituting a tenantry possessed of capital and who would be a greater security for the payment of rent. The Reverend Thomas Armstrong, a Presbyterian minister, in his account of his stay in Connacht suggested that

HAD THE process been carried on in a much more moderate way, it might have done well. But, apart from the hardships inflicted on those who were so rudely and ruthlessly driven from their dwellings, the overgrown farm system did not prove a success. The grazier or gentleman farmer is all very well, but it would be better for the country at large had a substantial yeomanry been created, who could live in reasonable comfort with their families on farms of a much smaller size than that aimed at by this 'clearing system'. The mode of carrying out clearings was such as to leave a sting of bitterness in the hearts of the evicted, which they carried to other lands, and still rankles in their breasts. I have seen crowds of peasantry, as they were about to take their seats on the long Bianconi car, kneel down in the open street of Ballina, and invoke the direst curses on those who had forced them into exile. 'Going with a vengeance' became a proverb, which subsequently was, with a certain hope and expectation, turned into 'coming with a vengeance'.

A young peasant in my neighbourhood had emigrated, but not exactly in the circumstances described, as his father had remained in occupation of the farm. One day a letter came from the son, and as the old man could not read he brought it to his landlord to read it for him. After the usual preliminaries, the letter goes on: 'Dear Father, pay no more rent. I belong to a party of ninety thousand Fenians, and we are about to land in Ireland to exterminate the landlords. The first man I will shoot is Captain ———', the gentleman who was reading the letter, and who did not deserve such a doom, as he was proverbially not only a just and fair, but a kind and indulgent landlord. I knew him well.

A splendid opportunity was at this time presented of settling or colonising the west of Ireland. Vast tracts were unoccupied and left to waste and desolation, which might have been re-peopled with a better class than before, without risk or danger. There were no claimants for the lands, for the former occupiers had disappeared and left no representatives to claim the succession. I urged the landlords to avail themselves of the situation, and they were willing enough. Several came from Ulster and Scotland to explore the country, and found they could readily get land on very low terms, and at long leases. But one fatal obstacle lay in the way: there were no farm buildings. The Scotchmen would not do without 'a steading', but they would not expend their capital on stone and lime. The landlords were too poor to provide the requisite structure, and so the project fell through. Some of the gentry who were able to do what was required would not. With a strange infatuation they dreaded the advent of a race of sturdy and independent men, who would not stand hat in hand to them nor crouch at the office door in subdued servility. They were told by these, 'We will pay a fair rent, but we will not be serfs. We wish to live with our families in decent comfort, in good houses, and in a way such as human beings ought to do', and so on. This the proud aristocrat could not brook.

I was greatly disappointed. A dream, not a fanciful one, but quite feasible, was dispelled. The chance was gone. Very speedily the population began to increase and multiply with marvellous, yet quite Irish rapidity. The lands were re-occupied, and the hope of a Protestant settlement of Connaught utterly gone.

Fenianism was the great talking point of the mid-sixties. The failure of Mitchel and Smith O'Brien in '48 did not deter the Irish revolutionaries, and while England was busy putting down the Indian Mutiny in 1857–8, James Stephens, who had taken part in the abortive attempt at insurrection at Ballingarry, established a secret society, the Phoenix Society, in the south of Ireland. The society collapsed in '58 following government moves against it, but it was replaced by another, better organised one, the Fenian Brotherhood.

This organisation was established simultaneously in Ireland and in America. At home, Stephens founded a newspaper, the *Irish People,* to preach his doctrine of revolution, while in America, after the end of the civil war in 1865, many Irish-Americans pledged to use the military skills they had acquired in a war of attrition against England. The Catholic Church in Ireland denounced Fenianism, and it was widely believed that the government spies had penetrated all its circles; but the strength of the organisation's American wing and the air of mystery surrounding it at home led to daily rumours of an imminent revolution. William Barry toured Ireland in 1865, some time before Stephen's arrest, and in his book *A Walking Tour in Ireland,* he remarked:

THE FENIAN movement naturally led me to dwell a good deal on its causes and consequences. Though all classes with whom I came in contact concurred in condemning the actions of the Fenians, yet there nevertheless existed even among educated men of the middle class a deep-seated feeling of discontent, of the most undefined and undefinable kind. Vaguely did they talk. Sometimes Ireland was not an integral part of the Queen's dominions, and should be governed differently; again the Queen should come often and the Prince and Princess of Wales. But whatever the form of expression it was rarely one of contentment. This circumstance I thought a fatal symptom. It would seem to show or illustrate

Pursuit of Fenians in Tipperary, 1867

that the lower orders of society must have some real cause for discontent, though it may be difficult to state or realise them. At all events it should not be taken for granted that because the Fenians have not broken out into open rebellion, therefore their numbers will fade away and their strength through very inaction become powerless. I consider the most dangerous sign to be that by no taunts of cowardice or want of patriotism, or threats, or menaces, from the more violent of their own party, they have been induced to measure their power with the constabulary and military. If so we should have known and clearly ascertained their power and its results. But it may be that the

Fenians are biding their time, and awaiting a more favourable period for action. The best way to disarm them would be by the introduction of legislative measures calculated as far as possible to ameliorate the present condition of the people. The landlords where necessary should be empowered to grant leases, and the value of improvements should be allowed to the tenant, and larger farms should be created, so as to give rise to a better class of farmers . . .

It is said that James Stephens, the Head Centre of the Fenians, has travelled throughout Ireland, visiting every village. I can scarcely believe it, for being, even as his enemies admit, an honest, though a mistaken man, I think if so he would abandon his insane attempt at rebellion. At all events, if the other centres, his dupes, would do as I have done, and walk around Ireland, they would feel convinced of the folly of their proceedings. Neither as regards geographical limits, nor population, nor size of cities or towns, nor natural fastnesses, is Ireland at all capable of coping with the strength of England. *The thing can't be done.*

The Fenians had the support of a high proportion of both the rural labourers and the unskilled workers of the towns. These classes had suffered great hardship in the years following the great famine. The cottiers had been reduced to labourers dependent on a money wage by the reluctance of the farmers to give them plots of land; many of them headed for the towns to increase the numbers of unskilled, and largely unwanted industrial workers. Fenianism thrived on their discontent.

The Fenian revolt, when it eventually happened in '67, ended in dismal failure. Even though the Fenians may not have had the support of the majority of Irishmen, there was a general outcry in Ireland at the severity of the sentences imposed on the captured rank and file of the movement. Dr James Macaulay, in his book, *Ireland in 1872—A Tour of Observation,* wrote:

HAVING REFERRED to convict prisons, I wish to say a few words about the Fenian prisoners, some of whom are still retained in penal servitude in England. Any account of Ireland in 1872 would be imperfect without taking notice of the strong feeling manifested as to the retention of these prisoners . . .

Fenian prisoners being escorted through the yard of Dublin Castle

The general feeling throughout Ireland is that these are political prisoners; and though this feeling is erroneous, it is not the less powerful in keeping up disaffection towards England. To treat political prisoners with the same severity as common felons is against the usage of civilised nations, and is regarded, in the case of these prisoners, as a wrong to Ireland. These prisoners have apparently been treated with exceptional harshness. I forbear from saying anything about the case of Reddin, who has brought an action-at-law against the prison authorities and medical officers for cruelty. He is now free, after undergoing his full sentence of five years. If he had been a common felon, he would probably have had his time shortened, and his sentence alleviated. The case of Davitt is even more painful. He is a maimed man, with one arm, and has been injured by forced labours which humanity would have spared him. His sentence of fifteen years was not so much for the heinousness of his crime, selling or purchasing arms, as 'to be a warning to others', as the Chief Justice said. If the statements made by Reddin and Davitt, which have been widely circulated in Ireland, have the least foundation in truth, there has been cruel severity exercised, and the alleged treatment of these convicts by the prison officials is a scandal demanding investigation.

The feeling of indignation among the people is very deep, and there will be no peace while enquiry is refused. Meetings are held, not only in Ireland, but in the great towns of England where Irishmen can meet in large numbers. The appeals are in temperate language, and I must avow that they are in themselves just and reasonable. Why should the few followers be retained, when the more guilty leaders have been released? The petitions for amnesty have been signed by larger numbers than any petition since the time of Catholic emancipation, and magistrates, clergy, and leading gentry and merchants, have presented addresses pleading for clemency. The majesty of law has been fully vindicated in the severity of the sentences, and pardon may be extended without any danger to public peace, and without offering the least encouragement to disloyalty. Mr Gladstone once had the matter before him, on the appeal of the late Mr Maguire of Cork. He referred to the Home Office, and was told that the treatment was only that to which all convicts were subject. If this is the case, there is the more need of public inquiry; for the treatment of some of these prisoners has been a disgrace to English justice and to common humanity.

THE STRUGGLE FOR THE
LAND

HOME RULE was overshadowed by the agrarian question. The Land Act of 1870 was not enough to solve the land question, for it provided no machinery for determining fair rents. At the suggestion of Michael Davitt, a Fenian, the farmers of the west of Ireland joined together in an organisation which they called the 'Land League'. Davitt explained his reasons for throwing in his lot with the tenantry:

HUMBLE AND obscure though my origins may be—the son of an Irish peasant who was refused shelter in an Irish workhouse by an Irish landlord, the son of an Irish mother who had to beg through English streets for me—humble as that origin may be, the memory of my mother made me swear (that) Irish landlords and English misgovernment in Ireland shall find in me a sleepless and incessant opponent.

There was great need for an organisation such as Davitt founded. The years 1877 to 1882 saw agricultural depression, and evictions became more and more frequent. Furthermore, the tenant farmers had hitherto accepted that the landlord was always entitled to his rent. As an emigrant farmer told New York's *Irish World* in 1880:

THE THOUGHT NEVER possessed them (the tenant farmers) that they had the greatest and only just claims to the land . . . or that they would be justified in demanding from the land robber

158

any part of the hereditary privileges he had so long mercilessly held.

Under the Land League, 'the land for the people' became the great slogan of rural Ireland. Parnell's beautiful sister, Fanny, wrote the Marseillaise of the movement:

> Oh, by the God who made us all—
> The Seigneur and the serf—
> Rise up! and swear this day to hold
> Your own green Irish turf;
> Rise up! and plant your feet as men
> Where now you crawl as slaves,
> And make the harvest fields your camps,
> Or make of them your graves.

The Land League found one effective way to curb the power of the landlords, and in so doing added a new word to the English language. Bernard H. Becker, special commissioner of the *Daily News,* saw how it worked, and wrote about it in his book, *Disturbed Ireland,* which was published in 1881:

THE CONDITION of Mr Boycott and his family has undergone not the slightest amelioration since he last week wrote a statement of his case to a daily contemporary. In fact, he is in many respects worse off. It will be recollected that about a month ago a process-server and his escort retreated on Lough Mask House, followed by a mob, and that on the following day all the farm servants were ordered to leave Mr Boycott's employment. I may mention that Mr Boycott is a Norfolk man, the son of a clergyman, and was formerly an officer in the 39th Regiment. On his marriage he settled on the Island of Achill, near here, and farmed there until he was offered some land agencies, which occupied so much of his time that he, after some twenty years' residence in Achill, elected to take a farm on the mainland. For seven years he has farmed at Lough Mask, acting also as Lord Erne's agent. He has on his own account had a few difficulties with his work-people; but these were tided over by concessions on his part, and all went smoothly till the serving of notices upon Lord Erne's tenants. All the

Attack on a process server during the Land League agitation

weight of the tenants' vengeance has fallen upon the unfortunate agent, whom the irritated people declare they will 'hunt out of the country'. The position is an extraordinary one. During his period of occupation Mr Boycott has laid out a great deal of money on his farm, has improved the roads, and made turnips and other root crops to grow where none grew before. But the countryside has struck against him, and he is now actually in a state of siege.

Personally attended by an armed escort everywhere, he has a garrison of ten constables on his premises, some established in a hut, and the rest in that part of Lough Mask House adjacent to the old castle. Garrisoned at home and escorted abroad, Mr Boycott and his family are now reduced to one female domestic. Everybody else has gone away, protesting sorrow, but alleging that the power brought to bear upon them was greater than they could resist. Farm labourers, workmen, herdsmen, stablemen, all went long ago, leaving the corn standing, the horses in the stable, the sheep in the field, the turnips, swedes, carrots, and potatoes in the ground, where I saw them yesterday. Last Tuesday the laundress refused to wash for the family any longer, the baker in Ballinrobe is afraid to supply them with bread, and the butcher fears to send them meat. The state of siege is perfect.

When the strike first began Mr Boycott went bravely to work with his family, setting the young ladies to reaping and binding, and looking after the beasts and sheep himself. But the struggle is nearly at an end now. Mr Boycott has sold some of his stock; but he can neither sell his crop to anybody else, nor, as they say in the north of England, 'win' it for himself. There remains in the ground at least five hundred pounds worth of potatoes and other root crops, and the owner has no possible means of doing anything with them. Nor, I am assured on trustworthy authority, would any human being buy them at any price; nor, if any such person were found, would he be able to find any labourer to touch any manner of work on the spot under the ban. By an impalpable and invisible power it is decreed that Mr Boycott shall be 'hunted out', and it is more than doubtful whether he will, under existing circumstances, be able to stand against it. He is unquestionably a brave and resolute man, but there is too much reason to believe that without his garrison and escort his life would not be worth an hour's purchase.

There are few fairer prospects than that from the steps of Lough Mask House, a moderately comfortable and unpretending edifice, not quite so good as a large farmer's homestead in England. But the potatoes will rot in the ground, and the cattle will go astray, for not a soul in Ballinrobe country dare touch a spade for Mr Boycott. Personally he is protected, but no woman in Ballinrobe would dream of washing him a cravat or making him a loaf. All the people have to say is that they are sorry, but that they 'dare not'. Hence either Mr Boycott, with an escort armed to the teeth, or his wife without an escort—for the people would not harm her—must go to Ballinrobe after putting a horse in the shafts themselves, buy what they can and bring it home. Everybody advises them to leave the country; but the answer of the besieged agent is simply this: 'I can hardly desert Lord Erne, and, moreover, my own property is sunk in this place.' It is very like asking a man to give up work and go abroad for the benefit of his health. He cannot sacrifice his occupation and his property.

There is very little doubt that this unfortunate gentleman has been selected as a victim whose fate may strike terror into others. Judging from what I hear, there is a sort of general determination to frighten the landlords. Only a few nights ago a man went into a store at Longford and said openly, 'My landlord has processed me for the last four or five years; but he hasn't processed me this year, and the divil thank him for that same.'

Captain Boycott enlisted the help of the cavalry and of some northern Orangemen in his effort to save his crops. The scheme was not very successful however. Becker again:

TO DO JUSTICE to the Ulstermen they displayed a great deal of earnestness at Lough Mask House this morning. In the midst of a hurricane a large number of them went bravely out to a potato field and worked with a conscience at getting out the national vegetables, which ran a risk of being completely spoiled by the rain. The potatoes, however, might, as Mr Boycott opined, have been spoiled if they remained in the ground, and might as well be ruined in one way as the other. The remainder of the Orangemen when I saw them, were busy in the barn with a so-called 'Tiny' threshing machine, threshing Mr Boycott's oats with all the serious and solemn purpose befitting their task. Nothing could have been more dreary and wretched than the entire proceedings. Mr Boycott himself had discarded his martial array of yesterday, and appeared in a herdsman's overcoat of venerable age, and, as he grasped a crook instead of a double-barrelled gun, looked every inch a patriarch. He exhibits no profuse gratitude towards the officious persons who have come to help him, thinking probably that he would have been nearly as well without them. Thanks to his obstructive assistants, he is almost overwhelmed with sympathisers gifted by nature with tremendous appetites. Keen-eyed officers detect the mutton-bones which tell of unauthorised ovicide, and 'clutches' of geese and chickens vanish as if by magic. There will be a fearful bill for somebody to pay when the whole business is over, whenever that may be.

From every quarter I hear acts of the so-called 'staunchness' of the population. When Captain Tomkinson went over to Claremorris yesterday with dragoons to convey the carts and other impediments of the Ulster division, it happened that one of the cart-horses lost a shoe. Will it be believed that it was necessary to delude the only blacksmith who could be captured with a story that the animal belonged to the Army Service Corps? Simple and artless, the Claremorris blacksmith made the shoe: but before he could put it on he was 'infawrrumd' that the beast he was working for was in an Ulster cart. Down fell the hammer, the nails, and the shoe. The blacksmith was immovable; not a blow more would he strike for love or money; nor would any blacksmith for miles around this place. At last the shoe was got on the horse's foot among the military and police; but not a soul belonging to this

Departure of the boycott volunteers from Lough Mask House

Troops escorting boycott relief volunteers from Lough Mask to Ballinrobe

part of the country would drive a cart at any price.

All this appears to point to the conclusion that when Mr Boycott's potatoes, turnips and mangolds are got in, and his oats are threshed out, when his sheep are either sold or devoured on the spot by his hungry defenders, he will accompany the Orangemen on their return march, at least to the nearest railway station. That neither he nor his auxiliaries would be safe for a single hour after the departure of the military is certain, and the expense of maintaining a huge garrison in Ballinrobe will therefore of necessity continue until the last potato is dug and the last turnip pulled.

Eventually, Boycott fled: the Land Leaguers' new policy had proved its efficacy.

J. L. Joynes, an assistant master at Eton, and a Land League supporter, came to Ireland in 1882, and afterwards wrote a book called *The Adventures of a Tourist in Ireland*. They were not all pleasant adventures: Mr Joynes was reminded of the tense state of the country by an incident in which he found himself involved at Loughrea, in county Galway.

A stringent coercion act had been passed following the assassination of Chief Secretary Lord Frederick Cavendish, and Mr Burke, the Under Secretary, by a group called the Invincibles in Dublin's Phoenix Park. The Invincibles numbered about thirty, and neither Home Rulers nor Land League farmers had anything to do with them; yet the coercion act was administered 'to the hilt', in Parnell's phrase, as Mr Joynes found out:

WE SAW NOTHING remarkable by the way, except a police hut erected at the roadside for the better protection of those who go out from and come into Loughrea. These police huts on the one side and the Land League huts on the other make quite a new feature in the scenery, partly resembling the cabmen's shelters which may be seen in the streets of London.

Moralising on these huts and their causes and objects, we drove into the village of Loughrea, and immediately noticed that here the police were even more plentiful than at the railway stations. Not for an instant supposing this fact had any connection with our arrival, we drove up to the door of the hotel and dismounted from our car. To our horror we then discovered that these numerous police were all converging upon one common centre, and that we ourselves were occupying that unenviable position. A sub-inspector in plain clothes suddenly advanced and informed us that we were arrested under the Prevention of Crime Act, and must instantly resume our seats on the car, in order to drive to a very different destination from that which we had proposed to ourselves when we started. It was useless to protest, and to ask at least to be told on what charge we were arrested. The only answer vouchsafed was, 'Get up instantly into the car.' There was nothing for it but to comply, so we climbed into our seats again. Two policemen with loaded rifles took their seats beside us; a procession of similarly armed constables walked before, behind, and on each side of us, and at the slow pace of a military funeral we proceeded through the main street of the village, a sight for all beholders.

Huts provided by the Land League for evicted tenants

The people of the place, however, were too well accustomed to such sights to display much emotion, although they sympathised with any new victim who had the misfortune to fall into the clutch of their oppressors. We arrived at the police barracks and were placed in a small room, furnished with a table and a form, and with strong iron bars to its window. Here our pockets were carefully searched for papers, and a minute examination of our luggage was made. In mine, besides the 'flannels', they made the discovery of six clean white linen shirts, and this at once aroused their strongest suspicion. They asked me if I had supposed that it would be possible to get a shirt washed in Ireland, and the question was certainly most apposite to the occasion, for in this zealous search for treasonable documents they thrust their dirty fingers into every fold of the aforesaid shirts, and made their speedy washing a thing of primary necessity. Having collected every scrap of paper that was to be found, they proceeded to examine their spoils. I was asked if I denied the authorship of a pamphlet on the land question which had been put into my hands in Dublin, and which I had not yet had time to read. This I accordingly did, and the statement was duly recorded. The sub-inspector and a constable,

166

one after the other, read through every one of our private letters and diaries and notebooks, and with some difficulty and much solemnity managed to spell out between them the only thing I was ashamed of—viz. some verses I had jotted down on a scrap of paper in imitation of the Irish national songs. When this was over, the sub-inspector departed, taking all our documents with him, and leaving us in the charge of a couple of constables. We were informed that as soon as a magistrate could be obtained our case should be tried before him, but when this would be was problematical.

It was now eight o'clock, and we had already been in custody for two hours and were getting hungry as well as tired. We asked if we might be guarded to the hotel, eat some dinner under police supervision, and return to the barracks in a less famished condition to defend our case before the magistrate when he should arrive. This was refused, so we modified our demands, and asked to be supplied with some bread and water, thinking that this, at least, was orthodox prison fare. Even this, however, could not be allowed, and our only resource was to try to forget our hunger, and to amuse ourselves as best we might by alternately sitting on our form and looking through the bars of our window into the court-yard. At last a policeman,

An eviction scene in county Wexford in the 1880s

A PLAN OF CAMPAIGN.

A MEMO. FOR THE COUNTRY.

HOW TO MEET THE NOVEMBER DEMAND.

HOW SHOULD THE FUND BE EMPLOYED?

THE ASSISTANCE OF THE NATIONAL LEAGUE.

THE LANDLORD'S REMEDIES.

EJECTMENT

DISTRESS

SALE.

BANKRUPTCY PROCEEDINGS

PUBLIC SYMPATHY.

whom I wish to take this opportunity of thanking, took pity on us, and procured at his own expense a glass of milk for each of us, and thus refreshed we hoped to be able shortly to face the magistrate. He was a long time coming however—and time passes slowly to prisoners—but before he came we were allowed an interview with our late driver, who had come to the police station with the double object of getting his pay and expressing his sympathy. He lamented over our misfortune, and earnestly hoped that we should soon be released; but there was no saying what the police might or might not do. This was cheering, but we could only wait. At nine o'clock Mr Byrne arrived, the resident magistrate for the district, and informed us that it was by the merest chance that he was in the neighbourhood, and that otherwise we should have been necessarily locked up all night. Here was a great subject of congratulation. Meanwhile preparations were made for our formal trial, for everything must be done regularly even under Coercion Acts, and all the evidence must be taken down in full on regular printed forms, of which there were none at hand, but which could not be replaced by ordinary foolscap paper. While these forms were being sent for, I made an informal statement of my aim and object in travelling through the country, and disclaimed all intention of committing an outrage at Loughrea, giving references to persons in authority which could be verified by the letters which the police had abstracted from me. Mr Byrne was evidently anxious to get rid of us, and when the forms at last arrived he asked of the sub-inspector if, after having read our letters and listened to my statement, he still entertained suspicions of our criminal intent. To this he replied in the negative, and the magistrate had nothing more to do than to discharge us and express his regret for our arrest, after which we were free to return to our hotel. I asked Mr Byrne to give me a letter to prevent the recurrence of such an unpleasant episode, and this he said he would do; but when I received a letter from him later in the evening it only stated that he thought this sort of safe-conduct would be unnecessary. So the prospect was not very pleasant.

The decline in population made it possible for many farmers to increase the size of their holdings in the years following the famine. Between 1849 and 1880, five million acres, almost twenty-five per cent of the area of Ireland, were sold under the Encumbered Estates Act to more solvent landlords, many of whom attempted consolidation and drainage. James Macaulay, in his *Tour of Observation,* remarked that even allowing for these improvements the condition of Irish agriculture was, in the main, very backward. He blamed 'the careless, indolent habits of the people' for this. He wrote:

THE MOST SUPERFICIAL observer must be astonished at the neglect and waste of natural resources. Even in the pasture lands, in which Ireland most excels, the spontaneous liberality of the soil seems to induce the greater indolence and carelessness. The aid of art has been little used in laying down land to grass, for it is only recently that the trade in grass seeds has assumed any dimensions. Even haymaking, as generally conducted, is a slovenly operation, though labour has been so abundant. Cut too late, I saw the grass often left in small cocks, to be drenched by the autumn rains. A good sweet haystack is the exception, not the rule, on an Irish farm.

I never saw such a country for weeds. I saw two men in a field with scythes mowing down ragwort! Had I been travelling afoot or in a car, and not in a railway carriage, I would have sought an explanation of so strange a sight. Had the ragwort been sown as a crop it could hardly have been closer, so as actually to be mown with scythes. Is it used as fodder for any Irish animal? I suspect it was only an extreme illustration of the miserable state of the agriculture too common in Ireland. The amount of weeds is a national disgrace. It is not uncommon to see a ton of weeds in a dozen tons of hay. Many a field has more weeds than a whole parish in England. Small tenants keep land without laying it down with grass seeds, and it becomes the receptacle for all the floating weeds of the district, and then spreads them far and wide. Even for green crops the land is seldom sufficiently cleaned. Smoking heaps of twitch and weeds are rarely seen. If the farmer would give a small reward to boys for heaps of weeds, as they used to do for heads of vermin, they could keep this nuisance under. Ragwort, for instance, can easily be pulled up by the roots in wet weather, and the boys from the work-house school would gladly attack a field for a trifling reward, and enjoy the fun of the bonfire that the heaps would make. But fields and roadsides are alike neglected, and weeds help to keep Ireland green but poor. I am sure it is no exaggeration to say that the direct loss to Ireland from weeds is above a million-and-a-half sterling. I have heard the loss estimated at nearly double that amount.

On the drainage of land, vast sums have been expended, and under good management with wonderful results. But even in land that has been drained, there is too-general carelessness in scouring ditches and keeping the outlets of drains clear. It is better to have no drains than drains choked. In many cases advances have been obtained by landlords for draining, but the neglect of the small tenants has made them regret the cost and trouble. In fact, draining is seldom of service except when the land is in the owner's hand or under efficient management.

The process server

Bad fences are also everywhere evident. The direct losses from the destruction of produce through this cause are enormous, and it is a constant source of litigation and ill will.

After the rejection by the Commons of the Home Rule bill brought in by Gladstone in 1886, Parnell framed a land bill which proposed that proceedings for the recovery of rent should be suspended on payment of half the rent and arrears. This bill too was rejected and as a result William O'Brien, one of Parnell's lieutenants, proposed the 'plan of campaign'. The plan was as follows: should the landlord refuse to accept the offer by the tenant of a fair rent, the money should be placed with a special committee; and should nothing come of negotiations between the landlord and that committee, the money should be used in a campaign against the landlord. Four years of fierce agitation followed the introduction of the plan of campaign. Evictions took place all over the country. Anne Marie de Bovet, a French visitor, wrote about them:

ORDINARY EVICTIONS are commonplace affairs, but those which are carried out at the price of a regular battle are worth going to see. The whole apparatus of the law is brought into play — police, infantry and cavalry. Barricading themselves in their houses, the inhabitants launch from the windows stones, broken pots, hot oil, and boiling water. To break in the doors a sort of battering-ram is employed, the walls are demolished stone by stone, men, women and children are dragged forth by main force, the movables are turned out, the doors and windows closed with planks, and sometimes the roof itself taken off to render the tenement uninhabitable. All this goes on amid the execrations of a yelling crowd, which an agitator or the priest of the parish inflames with well understood exhortations to abstain from violence. Nothing can be more distressing than these scenes, though my pity cannot be entirely withheld from the officers and soldiers, who frequently suffer severely in the discharge of their unpleasant duty. It is related that Lord Kenmare once found himself by accident present at an eviction of this kind. Seizing a hatchet which lay among the miserable furniture by the roadside, he knocked away the planks with which they had closed the doorway, gave the evicted family a handful of

172

money, and told them to re-enter. It was a natural movement of compassion; but after all he cannot allow hundreds of such families to appropriate his land without payment. It might be asked why these unfortunates allow things to proceed to such extremities? They had some excuse in the old days, when the mad competition for land forced rents up to an impossible figure; but these rents have been reduced again and again by legislation, which has placed the Irish tenant in a better position than any other in the world. But the old grudges remain, and are sedulously fostered by the League for political purposes, while the peasants cherish the ineradicable belief that the soil is theirs and not the landlords.

Mrs D. M. Craik, a much more sympathetic visitor than Anne Marie de Bovet, saw that for all the poverty, the tenantry had, under the Land League, achieved an independence of spirit, and that a great deal of Ireland's problems would be solved 'if only they were let alone'. Mrs Craik gave the following account of Gweedore, county Donegal, in her book *An Unknown Country*, published in 1887:

WE WERE RATHER quiet all the way to Gweedore, and then our spirits rose. Either the Atlantic storm never came, or we had driven out of its reach—the afternoon was beautiful. All who could walk proposed to start off along the moorland road towards Falcarragh; I following after, in the leisurely way out of which old folks who have courage to accept the fact that they cannot do like the young, may get so much pleasure and trouble nobody.

It was a very lonely road, and yet so sweet; with the shining line of lakes stretching all the way to Glen Veagh, the smooth sides of glittering Erigal, on the left hand, the long thread of mountain road visible for miles, and the fresh, pure air, half mountain, half bog; one has to go to Ireland to learn the wonderfully bracing properties of bog air, the same above the surface as its preservative qualities below. Walking became a pleasure instead of a weariness. For an hour I met not a creature, except a big cart-horse carrying a young man and woman, without a saddle. Her scarlet plaid was over her head, with its neatly-combed, glossy black hair, her bare feet dangled, and her arms were round the young man's waist. They might have been sweethearts, but looked

173

Glencolumbkille, county Donegal

more like brother and sister, jogging along so steady and so grave.

I sat on the low turf wall and watched them, thinking what a picture they made, and wondering, as one does wonder sometimes, how life goes on among people different to ourselves in habits and education; what they think of, what they talk about, and how difficult it is to judge of their feelings by our own. And yet one ought to try to understand and get near them; as I tried, by smiles and biscuits combined, to win some little ragamuffins who

174

were playing near two or three roadside cabins. One could scarcely tell whether they were boys or girls, their few clothes were so oddly heterogeneous. They hardly understood English, I thought, from the few words I got out of the biggest of them, but I managed to discover that they had seen a gentleman and three ladies walking up the road.

'If you see them again, go and speak to them, and say mother has gone home. Remember the words, mother—has—gone—home.'

The small individual—I think the bundle of rags contained a boy—nodded solemnly, and passed my last biscuit over to two lesser infants, who regarded it as if they had never seen such a thing before, and never attempted to eat it. Exceedingly doubtful as to how far I had been understood—though I afterwards found my message had been accurately and literally delivered—I spoke to a woman whom I met shortly after, and found that she had seen my party.

'Three young ladies and a gentleman. That's yer husband, maybe? He's pretty well on'—in years I suppose she meant—'like yerself.'

And she eyed me over, especially my stick, with simple kindliness, and slackened her brisk pace to keep beside me. She was a big, strong, middle-aged woman, in the usual frieze petticoat and bright-coloured shawl, with bare head and feet. But her clothes were whole, her face was clean and her hair tidy. She carried a large bundle and was evidently bound for a journey of a good many miles. We went on together, I putting my best foot forwards, but in vain.

'I'm going too fast for ye, ma'am. Ye see, I'm used to walking. An' my brogues'—glancing with sly humour at her bare feet—'my brogues don't wear out.'

I laughed, confessed my inferiority, and then we fell into a long talk. She spoke slowly and a little disjointedly, as if she had first to arrange her thoughts and then translate them into a foreign tongue. I do not attempt, never have attempted, to give the brogue; indeed, here I rarely found it. The 'stage' Irish, the unctuous Cork and Limerick accent, and the Dublin twang are not noticeable in Antrim, Derry, and Donegal, where the original Gaelic has been gradually changed into the English taught at National Schools. Many of the older generation speak only Irish, but the younger population know both languages, though, as with this woman, their English comes to them like a foreign tongue—slowly, but correctly . . .

We talked a good deal about the state of the country. 'It's been hard times

175

Left
A country kitchen

Below
Journeying on foot, c. 1899

with us for a long time,' she said, 'but things are mending a bit. Many of us have gone to America—there's no starving there. A kind English lady has been helping us in Donegal—the women, I mean—giving us work and paying for it. Maybe ye'll know her?'

'Mrs Ernest Hart', I suggested—glad to own that I did know her.

'Sure, that's the name. I don't work for her myself, but I know them as does. She pays them regularly, ye see. She's brought a little money into the counthry, and it's money we want; we're all so poor.'

Yet the woman never asked, or by her manner hinted in the smallest degree, that *I* should give her money. Nor did I—her air of sturdy independence would have made me ashamed to offer it.

She gave me, in her unconscious candour, much information about Donegal, and asked me no end of questions, after the simple fashion of country people, who take as much interest in you as they expect you to take in them; a refreshing change from the bitterly-learnt reticence—or indifference—of towns. And when I said I would not hinder her longer, as I could not walk as fast as she could, she regarded me with a tender pity that was amusing.

'I see ye can't. Ye're not as young now as ye have been, though ye're wearin' pretty well. Ye'd betther sit down a bit.'

Which I did, on a tempting bank of turf: and watched her down the road, with her free, springy step, and upright carriage, fit to be mother to half-a-dozen Donegal 'boys'—as no doubt she was. And I thought what splendid stuff these Irish peasants are made of, if only—to repeat what more than one compatriot said of them—'if only they were let alone'.

Not let alone in neglect; that is a totally different thing. And yet there are difficulties—incomprehensible in England, where, between the squire and his farm-labourer is a smooth succession of several ranks, each melting into the other, and continually meeting on mutual ground of help and kindliness. Education, too, is there a not impossible breaker of barriers. Sometimes the labourer's daughter becomes nurse or lady's maid at the hall, and the blacksmith's clever son has ere now been helped to school and college by the squire; and even come to sit at the squire's table. But such things are impossible, or held to be impossible in Ireland. What bond of union could there be, for instance, between this poor woman I met and Mrs Adair of Glen Veagh, with her five hundred miles of deer-park palings and her twenty thousand pounds spent in improvements at the castle? Did they meet—which

177

they are never likely to do—they would regard one another, and judge one another, like two beings out of different spheres, who scarcely owned a common humanity.

The gulf between upper and lower classes—of middle class there is almost none—is in Ireland enormous. The lower class can never bridge it. Will the upper class cross it to them? And how? God only knows. Certainly demagogues do *not* know. Nor do many of the 'gentry' of the last generation— who preserve the fatal traditions of the French aristocracy before the Revolution, and scarcely feel as if the common people were of the same flesh and blood as themselves. The only hope seems to be in the uprising of a new generation, with wider eyes and calmer judgment, who can hold out a helping hand to either side, teaching the one that 'the old order changeth, giving place to the new', and preaching to the other that justice between man and man, is due as much to the higher as to the lower stratum of society, and that the best of self-government consists in ruling one's self. There may then be some hope of Ireland's gaining that true freedom, which is only attainable by a prudent, peaceful, and law-abiding race . . .

There are landlords and landlords. No doubt Ireland has suffered cruelly from the worst type of that order, who, generation after generation, lived recklessly, ruinously, in their Castle Rackrents, till their impoverished descendants of today, with the same extravagant tastes, the same contemptible pride, ashamed of economy though not of debt, have found it impossible to maintain 'the family' in the only style which they consider its due. They therefore run away from what they dare not face; become permanent absentees, and spend in England or abroad the money they get out of the estate; keeping up the credit of owning property, but shirking alike its duties and responsibilities. Such landlords—and the Encumbered Estates Court has long proved how many there are—spendthrift 'gentlemen', who have over-built, over-eaten, over-drunk themselves, and then racked their tenants to supply their own extravagances, have been the curse of Ireland. They deserve no mercy, only strict justice.

But there is another class who deserve justice also, and do not always get it, being included in the common howl against 'landlordism', which is now sowing in Ireland all the seeds of civil war—I mean the 'good old Irish gentleman' who has lived on his estate, as his father lived before him, spent all his money there, done his best for his tenants, exacted from them no more than his due, and shown an example of thrift, industry, kindliness, and charity.

In certain parts of Ulster the tenants were remarkably well off. The farm Edwin Trueman visited in 1889 in Fermanagh, and which he described in his book, *Notes on a Trip to Ireland,* was a model one with few equals anywhere in the country:

THE SUN WAS sinking in the far west, and there was hardly a breath of air to fan the heated brows of the labourers who were busily engaged in securing the hay-harvest in the neatly-mown fields by the side of the highway we traversed. Seated on an embankment, intently watching a party of these labourers, who could be easily overlooked from this elevated position, although a considerable distance away, we found old Robert Wilson—or 'Robin', as he is familiarly termed—the thrifty occupier of Gola Abbey, and one of the most successful farmers in the neighbourhood. In real Irish fashion and the genuine brogue, he bid us welcome to his hospitable homestead. Round each of his knees we noticed that the old man had tied a red handkerchief, and we learnt with sorrow that he was so afflicted with rheumatism, that he was totally unable to walk, and

Dancing in the kitchen

had been carried from the house to the position he then occupied. Otherwise, 'Robin' Wilson, although over ninety years of age, seemed to be a hale and hearty specimen of the sturdy Irish race. He cordially invited us to 'look round' the ancient place where he was born, and seemed from the way in which he stated it, quite proud of the fact that his landlord was 'Sur' Charles King, Bart., of Corrard and London. We *did* 'look round', and 'sure enough' some of the foundations of the old abbey were still to be seen, on which had been built hundreds of years before the residence of one of the old Irish Kings, and which afterwards was used as an abbey by the monks. The place was evidently familiar to Mr Kaye, who pointed out to us a butter churn, worked in a novel manner by horse-power. We found that 'Robin' was the owner of a large number of stock, and that he made butter in such large quantities, that to churn by hand was out of the question. The butter is sent in tubs or firkins to the market at Enniskillen or Lisbellaw, and the old man assured us that it was not at all 'salt', as we are apt to get it very often when retailed in England. We were afterwards told that Mr Wilson's labourers are each allowed at dinner a quarter of a pound of butter, which is mixed with their potatoes, and serves the purpose of gravy instead of bacon in summer; bacon being almost universally used in all the country districts of Ireland in lieu of fresh meat. While we were 'exploring' the exterior of the house, Mr Wilson's two daughters, who had been informed of our arrival, had transferred the old man from the place where we first found him into a seat in the chimney corner, and had made certain preparations to do honour to their unexpected guests. And one or two words here with respect to the Misses Wilson. Delicate though the subject is, I do not think I should be justified in passing it over in silence. They were not very young, possibly between thirty and forty, but womanly and intelligent. It is equally certain that they knew how to work; and though they flitted about with bare feet, attending to the wants of their multitudinous live stock, until I felt disposed to pity them, as I would some street 'Arab', I was glad to learn that they discarded shoes solely because they considered them both inconvenient and unnecessary, except on special occasions. These 'special occasions' were usually on Sundays, when they attended our kind clerical friend's little church as neat and prim as any lady in the land. It was even whispered in the locality that if they left the old man's roof, as another sister had done, the 'marriage portion' would not be of a character to be despised. Having said this much, we will return to 'old

180

Robin' in the chimney corner, where he was snugly seated when we entered the kitchen, as I suppose it would be called. The floor of this room was the bare earth, and on the hearth was burning a large turf fire, the smoke from which ascended and made its escape from the house by way of an open chimney of extraordinary dimensions. Hams and bacon in abundance ornamented the walls and ceiling of the kitchen, as though this kind of provision had been stored up in anticipation of either a lengthened siege of the place, or to avoid a possible scarcity in the winter season. Presently we were invited into the parlour, which was a strange contrast to the living-room, and was really a comfortably nicely furnished apartment. Glasses were placed before us, and a large jug of Irish cream. A bottle containing a supply of the 'dear old cratur' was also forthcoming, and we were cordially bidden to 'improve' the contents of the jug by adding just a 'wee dhrap'. However, the cream taken from the milk of the Kerry cow is so thick that it needs no 'improvement', so that the majority of us preferred to taste it in its native purity, and found it extremely palatable, with the addition of a little sugar. As the long summer's day was fast drawing to a close, our visit to Gola Abbey was necessarily of brief duration; and bidding all its hospitable inmates a hearty good-bye, we made the best of our way back to Derrybrusk for the night.

Robin Wilson obviously hadn't taken advantage of the Ashbourne Act of 1885 through which a tenant could be loaned part or the whole of the money necessary to buy his farm from the landlord at four per cent over forty-nine years. The landlord's agreement to sell was, however, necessary, and consequently the Act affected only a small number of tenants. (Most of the land purchase came after the Wyndham Act of 1903.) Nevertheless, the Ashbourne Act was a step in the right direction, as was the creation of the Congested Districts Board in 1891 to develop agriculture along the western seaboard.

COUNTRY GENTLEMEN

THE POOR state of Irish farming in the Land League days was also noted by Terence McGrath in an interesting book called *Pictures from Ireland,* published in London in 1880. McGrath described the life of a 'gentleman farmer', one of those 'half-sirs' mentioned by Mr and Mrs Hall forty years previously.

MR HYACINTH O'CALLAGHAN of Gurtnamona, or 'Hycy' as he is called by his friends, has never repined at the fate that has made him a farmer. From the day when, in accordance with his father's will, he took possession of the hundred and fifty acres surrounding the small house of Gurtnamona, he has known no real sorrows, nor felt the unhappiness of an unsatisfied ambition. Not that his ambition soared to heights unknown to the average farmer. He wants a good price for his horse; a good profit on his heifers and sheep, and he has generally succeeded in obtaining both. When he entered into the occupation of Gurtnamona there was a considerable amount of tillage. But this did not suit Mr O'Callaghan's tastes. He has no intention, nor has he ever had any, of being a slave to his business. He wants a roof over his head, enough to share with a friend or friends, as the case may be, and a good horse to ride to hounds. So long as Gurtnamona gives him all three he is satisfied.

When Mr O'Callaghan was left the farm of Gurtnamona he came in for the lease alone. His father had not considered it necessary to leave him any money for the purchase of stock, and the problem of how to work the farm was not easy of solution. However, the bank was accommodating, and in return for the deposit of his lease in the bank safe, he has been granted permission to overdraw his account permanently to an amount sufficient to stock the farm. From that day to this Mr O'Callaghan has never quite known if he was solvent at any given moment; but he has bought and sold, hunted, shot, taken his part as steward of the neighbouring race meeting, and generally carried himself with as light a heart as if Gurtnamona were his own and no half-yearly settlement of interest on overdrafts were ever entered in his bank-book.

Mr O'Callaghan is a thorough sportsman. From the time when he escaped from the nursery he has devoted himself heartily to the destruction of fish, flesh, and fowl. He has caught everything from a 'pinkeen' to a salmon, shot everything from a wren to a wild goose, and hunted everything from the mouse in the corn-stack to the fox in the gorse cover. See him open the stomach of his first trout, and, placing the contents in a glass of clear water, note the fly most tempting for that day, and you can understand one of the elements of his success. He is a dead shot; but as a shooting man his conduct is not above reproach, and his ideas about boundaries are hazy. A certain off-handed carelessness as to the sacredness of his neighbour's preserves has caused some irritation from time to time; and when he exterminated the covey of thirteen partridges carefully preserved for Mr Lloyd's friends, who were to shoot the following day, that gentleman would have taken serious notice of the matter had a connection of his not been a candidate for the appointment of petty-sessions clerk and Mr O'Callaghan's cousin one of the magistrates with whom the appointment rested.

But the true magnet that has drawn Mr O'Callaghan and most of his friends towards the occupation of a stock farmer is the branch of his business connected with the making and selling of horses. Here he feels that his occupation is that of a gentleman. From the purchase of the two brown colts at Cahirmee farm to their sale two years after at Ballinasloe as trained hunters the speculation has been an abiding source of pleasure. Their training was a pastime, and the profit on their sale more than sufficient to pay for his subscription to the county hounds, the pink that made so brave a show at the cover-side, and the incidental expenses of the hunting season.

Mr O'Callaghan is hospitable, and his friends, Kelly of Kelly's Grove, French of Clonlough, O'Malley of Stabletown, and three or four other gallant sportsmen of the same kidney, are always welcome, as he is to their

A jaunting car

houses. The grass that straggles over the neglected gravel of the approach, and the flowering dandelions that flourish upon it in spite of passing cart-wheels and horses' hoofs, show that neatness is not to be counted among his virtues. A scraggy cotoneaster, torn from its support against the wall, falls across the open halldoor, but has been roughly hoisted to a level with the top by a piece of rope made fast to a wall-hook above. At the door lies Tiger, a good specimen of the bull-terrier, and two handsome Gordon setters walk in and out at their own sweet will. Mr O'Callaghan's friends understand the ways of the house, and, having left their horses in the yard, have no fear of the dogs, who know them all, but walk straight into the room that serves at once as drawing-room, dining-room, and smoking-room. On the walls hang some sporting prints and a lithograph copy of the portrait presented to the master of the hounds by the members of the hunt. On the sideboard is a miscellaneous collection of old newspapers, almanacs, some railway novels, and a moth-eaten stuffed snipe of abnormal size. We will not look into the corners or behind the writing-desk, nor yet too closely under the dining-table, for sooth to say, Mr O'Callaghan is a careless man, and never observes the little heaps of dust and bread-crumbs in which each leg of the table is set. If he did, Biddy O'Shea, who cooks his unpretending dinners so satisfactorily and attends to his few household wants, would declare that he was 'no better than a prying Scotch steward, to go throublin' his head about little things in the house, when her heart was broke with work intirely'. As to the cookery, even Biddy declares that 'the masther' is reasonable.

'My dear fellow,' Mr O'Callaghan always observes to a person invited to dine at Gurtnamona for the first time, 'I don't go in for any of your new-fangled, nonsensical dishes. I'll give you a good piece of corned-beef and a wisp of cabbage, or a boiled goose with onion sauce. You shall have some ten-year-old Jameson's whiskey, and we will have a jolly good song and a chorus after dinner. So if that won't tempt you, do not come.'

Mr O'Callaghan is not a drunkard, though his brother Tom, when home on leave, warned him that he drank more than was good for him. He certainly is not anything like a total abstainer, and when he rode the Bellman colt up the steps of the 'grand' stand at Liscannor races, his enemies hinted that that extremely dangerous performance was the consequence of the champagne he had previously imbibed at the luncheon table underneath. But many young ladies present refused to regard the frolic as anything but an evidence of cool courage, while the delighted multitude outside the enclosure greeted the daring feat with roars of delight. At Punchestown, where many old friends are met, he shares a goodly number of glasses, and when the 'Irish money' is on in the right direction at Liverpool, he pleads guilty to a 'night of it' at his hotel in honour of the success.

How the farming pays with so very little supervision is a mystery to many. In reality it does not pay in the sense in which a hard-working farmer would use the word. The rent is low, and the profits enable Mr O'Callaghan to live from hand to mouth. He has been told that high feeding on the grass will make the pasture much more valuable, and stall-feeding with more tillage would greatly increase his income; but no cottier is really less progressive than he. Looking only for enough to afford him the beaten track of his amusements he does not contemplate any change that would entail greater trouble and possibly greater risk. He had some idea at one time of taking the farm at Croghan; but the herd, who as a matter of course went with the farm, bore so bad a character that he would not have him, and to dismiss him meant a deliberate courting of peril from which Mr O'Callaghan shrank; so he gave up the idea. With the country people around he is a favourite; never interfering in local affairs or politics, always ready to give if possible a helping hand at a fair, and constantly looking about for young horses, he and the people are on the most friendly terms. He certainly got a bad beating returning one night from Knockfad, where he had been dining with the other members of the hunt. He was confined to bed for a week, and would have sworn informations only that in the handsomest manner some of the party who had waylaid him waited upon him and explained that they had mistaken him for young Mr Blundel of Moyglass, who was to have driven home by that road but unfortunately went by another way. The explanation was quite satisfactory, and Mr O'Callaghan declared that he bore no malice for the mistake. On the hill opposite to Gurtnamona a large bonfire blazed the night of the first day on which he left the house, and he duly appreciated the compliment.

On questions of home politics he is profoundly ignorant, but he has an idea that a war would be a good thing in many ways. It would, he thinks, raise the price of cattle, and might give his brother Tom promotion. He takes but little interest in the land question as a means to enable him to purchase his farm. He feels quite contented as he is, and would laugh at the person who gravely proposed an increase of ten or twenty per cent to his rent for thirty-five years that he might find himself the owner in fee at the expiration of that time. Besides, Mr O'Callaghan's passion is fox-hunting, and being convinced that peasant-proprietary is inimical to that noble sport, he is prepared to oppose it to the bitter end.

Terence McGrath also left us a pen picture of the rural money-lender, or gombeen man. Despised as he often was as a social parasite and as a racketeer, the gombeen man nevertheless played an important role in the rural community of post-famine Ireland. He it was who advanced money for the rent, and by introducing credit facilities he enabled the people to purchase luxuries to which they had not been accustomed and to improve their diet by shopping more frequently. McGrath wrote:

MUCH ABUSED AS is James Foley, many of his neighbours know that but for his timely assistance when the landlord's rent or the shopkeeper's demand had to be met they would have been obliged to pay costs, and perhaps have suffered the horrors of eviction. James Foley has been a money-lender for many years. He began his career on returning from a successful migration to England, when a neighbour who required ten pounds offered to give him two pounds for the loan of that amount for six months. From that moment the die was cast, and, the sweets

Killarney in 1890

of discount once tasted, he turned his money month by month, spending nothing except what sufficed for his bare necessities, and working hard to add to his store, until at length he found himself in possession of a goodly sum and settled in a small farm—most of his labour being done as complimentary work by his numerous debtors and those who wished to stand well with the gombeen man in view of possible contingencies.

The discount charged by Foley is generally about thirty per cent, or one and sixpence in the pound for three months. Of course this is for well-assured sums, where the promissory note is given by two or three joint securities; but when more risky business is done the discount increases, until for small amounts as much as cent per cent has been paid in kind.

Not even the parish priest knows more family secrets than does James Foley. Among his best clients are the women, who barter in advance their eggs and butter for small loans to cover expenditure to which the husbands would strongly object. Half the produce of Biddy Brady's thirteen hens was duly handed over for an entire season in payment of the interest on a loan of five pounds, and Foley knew so well the average number of eggs that she could not cheat him of even six in a week. Biddy Brady does not like to tell her husband of that debt, for he is a respectable man and would disapprove of it highly. Indeed, his thrift was the cause of the drain going on in the income of the establishment; for he refused to permit his wife to buy a new cloak on the ground that her present one was not quite worn out, and such stinginess could not be tolerated by any woman of spirit. She has almost exhausted her ingenuity in accounting for the way by which she purchased the cloak; but the truth must come out one day, and then the cloak will be for a time a garment of sorrow.

Foley had established a large business before the National Bank opened a branch in the neighbouring town. Its advent at once deprived him of all the really solvent customers, who now borrowed at ten per cent the money for which they had hitherto paid thirty. But a large class still remains whose security is so doubtful that their credit is worthless. To men like these he still gives loans, watching his opportunity to obtain repayment. He rarely appeals to the law for the recovery of his money. So long as the people are allowed to pay by small instalments they honestly strive to pay their debts, and, the money yielding good interest, Foley is content to receive the smallest amount, the discount and premium being paid on the renewal. Though the establishment of a branch bank has deprived Foley of the most secure portion of his business, it has enabled him to increase his small loans tenfold. He is known in the bank as a solvent man, and the bills given to him are duly entered to his account; and as the bank will renew for him readily, he suffers no inconveniences from protracted payments.

Foley is a very regular attendant at fairs and markets. He may not have anything for sale, but he takes careful notes of the sales and purchases of his neighbours. He can tell to a lamb the stock in possession of every person around, and confounded Paddy Ellis, who refused his demand for the payment of an instalment on the ground that he handed over his oats to the landlord for rent, by telling him that he had the day before received five pounds fourteen for the oats in hard cash from a corn-dealer.

He sold all his litter of pigs on credit. The bargain was that ten shillings over the market price was to be paid by the purchaser; the money not to be paid until the pig had been resold. Tom Barry thought he did a good stroke of business when he fattened the pig and killed it for his own use, refusing to pay Foley. He defended the process for the amount, on the plea that as he had not re-sold the pig the time for payment had not come; but in this case ingenuity was not rewarded, for a decree was granted for the amount claimed.

A hard man is Foley when his money is in danger, and fearless as a hero in the recovery of a doubtful debt. Yet at times he has been lavish in his expenditure. In his success, as in his poverty, family affection has remained green and vigorous, and when his father was dying he determined that he should have a respectable wake. The old man watched the preparations with the keenest interest, and as his peaceful end approached he noted with a quiet pleasure the completion of the brown pall, ornamented with white satin cross and bows, that was to cover him while the funeral festivities were in progress. Everything was made tidy, and the candles already lit before he breathed his last, and for three nights the neighbours flocked to the house to pay the last mark of respect to the deceased. Helping themselves to tobacco and snuff from plates laid upon the legs and breast of the dead parent, and to whiskey, of which a plentiful supply was on the table, they sat round the room chatting and singing songs, or playing some romping game to keep up the spirits of the family; and James Foley noted with pride the numbers that assembled next day to accompany the funeral.

Many attempts have been made by the farmers of Killballyegan to secure

The marketplace in Cong, county Galway

for a son-in-law so 'warm' a man; but Foley feels that a wife would be a disturbing element in his business, and the cares of a money-lender are not conducive to the tender passion. He has therefore resisted all offers of alliance with his neighbours. Not even Betty Houlahan's two hundred pounds could tempt him; though at one time her parents fondly hoped that it would have been a match. Indeed the affair was in a fair way to a satisfactory arrangement, for a mutual friend had visited Foley and told him that on the day of the marriage the two hundred pounds would be placed in his hands in hard cash. Foley was so far tempted that he promised to go over the following day and pay a visit to the Houlahans. Great preparations were made to receive him, and Betty Houlahan appeared in a silk dress, determined to display her charms to the greatest advantage. But here she made what a huntsman would call a wrong cast. Foley was to be tempted by money, not charms, and the silk dress settled the matter. He made a rapid survey of Betty's attire: that silk dress must have cost six pounds and the kerchief fastened by a gorgeous brooch at least ten shillings more. The boots were unfitted for field work, and the general get-up more suited to the shop than the farm. Foley calculated that it would take at least the interest of her money to satisfy her wants, and in such a marriage he could not see his way to any profit; so the marriage fell through. He is now looked upon as a determined old bachelor; and as he has no near relatives, a cousin 'six o' kin' at present working as a farmer's boy, is looking forward to the time when he may step in for a valuable inheritance.

But Foley has no intention of leaving his money for the enrichment of his connections. He loves money for money's sake; and if he could take it with him he would require no other heaven. But as he cannot, he at least may secure to himself hereafter some benefit from the hard work of accumulation in this world. He has determined to leave the greater portion of his money to be expended in Masses for his soul, that his term of purgatory may thus be shortened; and the direction in which the remainder may be left will greatly depend upon the views of the person who writes his tardy will, when, at the last, his wearied brain will escape from the trouble of decision by assenting to the proposals of the neighbour who has hurriedly been called upon to inscribe his last will and testament.

NATIONAL MOVEMENTS

PARNELL, the main driving force behind both the Home Rule movement and the fight for the land, was somewhat neglected by the visitors to Ireland. Few of them seem to have met him—probably because he spent so much time in England—but the meetings his party held were attended by many curious travellers. Baron Mandat Grancey, in his book *Paddy at Home* published in 1887, obtained a pass to attend a meeting of the Protestant Home Rule Association, which was to be held in the middle-class suburb of Rathmines. On the previous day some students of Trinity College had pelted the Nationalist candidate with 'a dead cat, seventeen rotten eggs, one of which broke in the face of a courageous lady who had accompanied him on to the platform, and such a number of cabbage stalks that the most conscientious reporters were forced to give up the attempt to count them'. The students were expected to storm the Rathmines meeting, which is why the Baron went along.

A JAUNTING-CAR conveyed me in less than half an hour to the door of a very simple building, which is the Town Hall of Rathmines. If England's tutelage, complained of by the Lord Mayor, has only the effect of recalling to the minds of the municipal architects the simplicity of style they so frequently lose sight of at home, this tutelage can scarcely be considered absolutely injurious. The street is already blocked by the crowd. Apparently the police are under the impression that there will be some work for them, for a hundred policemen are grouped in one corner, ready to interfere when necessary, but content to look on for the present.

Some strong young men wearing a green badge act as stewards and guard the doors. Everyone desiring to enter must show a personal invitation. These cards have been sent out during the day. I have only an envelope signed by Mr Gray. At first, therefore, I encountered some difficulties, because the signature was almost illegible; but as soon as it was recognised, one of the stewards gave me a formidable slap on the shoulder, exclaiming: 'Bedad, sorr, with that name there isn't any door in Ireland that wouldn't be open to you!'

I explained to him that for the moment my sole ambition was to find a place where I could see well, and above all hear well. My friend at once told me to follow him; pushing through the crowd like a boar, hustling everyone that stood in his way, and in five minutes I find myself on the platform, two steps from the President, and quite close to a window; a very advantageous position, because, first of all, I could get a little air, and secondly, if the tumult became too serious, a small jump of seven or eight feet would enable me to gain a small side lane; and this I determined to do, if necessary, without the least hesitation, for it would be too stupid to allow myself to be knocked down by a Nationalist, wounded by a student, or simply led off to the station by a policeman, all for the honour of 'Ould Ireland', although my martyrdom could not help her in any way.

When I had once formed my plan of campaign, I began to look about me. There was evidently electricity in the air. The hall could hold about three or four hundred people; a hundred and fifty or two hundred were crowded in a small gallery above the door, yet formidable pressure still took place from time to time, and on each occasion a fresh stream of people penetrated into the hall, and the new arrivals pushed forward against those who had entered before them. It was intensely hot, and already a good many present had taken off their coats. In order to pass the time they yelled out a patriotic song, commencing with *God Save Ireland*, which was accompanied from the street by an orchestra composed of five or six fifes and as many drums.

A few minutes later, a grey-haired gentleman rose quite near to me and advanced to the front of the platform, where he was joined by a short, deformed man with long hair. I don't know where he came from. Instantly there was a great silence, and the former bowed to the assembly . . .

'Gentlemen', said he, 'seconded by my friend Abraham Shackleton, and in the name of the *Protestant Home Rule Association* I wish to ask your support for our candidate, Sir Thomas Esmonde, Baronet, who already represents the electoral division of South Dublin.'

This declaration was received with a tremendous noise. Everyone stood up, hats flew into the air, or were waved at the ends of enormous blackthorn sticks that are here called shillelahs, mouths opened like ovens, and gave vent to hurrahs that made the hall shake. The voters in the gallery thumped with all their force on the wooden balustrade, making it resound like a drum. My eyes were fixed on a short man, standing in front of me; he shouted and gesticulated so violently that I expected he would be seized with an epileptic fit. After a moment he evidently broke something in his throat, for with a despairing gesture he indicated that his voice would not come again, and, red as a tomato, he sank upon a bench to recover his strength.

The same accident probably happened to several others, for comparative silence ensued. Unfortunately, some one took advantage of it to cry: 'Boys! Three cheers for the Grand Old Man!'

The 'Grand Old Man' is Mr Gladstone. Some years ago they called him 'the old scoundrel'.

The quite novel idea of cheering 'the Grand Old Man' made everyone recover his strength. One gentleman in the gallery gave the signal by attempting to demolish the balustrade with his shillelah and the nine hurrahs broke out like a peal of thunder. Their enthusiasm was so great that when it ended one voice cried, 'Once more', and they recommenced.

But human strength has its limits and I saw with pleasure that they were nearly exhausted. The second volley of hurrahs was not so hearty as the first. At last their throats could only utter inarticulate sounds; in spite of the efforts betrayed by their distorted features aphony was rapidly approaching.

The orators grouped near to me on the platform evidently awaited this result. One of them rose and began to speak. He first alluded to the meddling of the Court with the elections. He had scarcely launched into his subject before a young man suddenly rose at the back of the hall. 'Long live the Queen! Down with the rebels!' he cried in a clear voice. Two or three other voices responded. It was the students who had just entered, but their arrangements were badly planned. Their adversaries had taken every precaution, and very few students had succeeded in slipping into the room.

The tempest was unchained, a forest of cudgels waved overhead. The students made an heroic defence, but in less than a minute they were overpowered, picked up and thrust out amidst growls resembling those of wild beasts.

However, the affair was not yet over. In the streets their friends attempted a diversion. The music which had recommenced ended in a despairing scream. A heavy blow had broken one musician's instrument in his face and the others took to flight. Some curious fights took place under my window; the combatants, so far as I could judge, seemed to display very serious and profound knowledge of the principles of the noble art of boxing, for in the twinkling of an eye I saw two or three noses broken. 'A very illigant foight! Is it not, sorr?' said one of my neighbours, addressing me; he evidently considered it would be a personal favour if I declared myself anti-Nationalist so that he might have the opportunity of commencing an equally 'illigant foight' with me. I took care not to give him this satisfaction; on the contrary, I declared that I thought the fight most 'illigant'.

Even the tragedy of the Parnell split and the great man's untimely death in

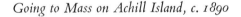

Going to Mass on Achill Island, c. 1890

1891 could not hold back the flood-tide of nationalism. For other influences were at work strengthening the character of Irish life and emphasising its distinctiveness. The Gaelic Athletic Association, founded in 1884, organised native sports on a nation-wide basis, while the Gaelic League, founded in 1893 by Douglas Hyde, later to become the first President of Ireland, had as its aim the revival of the Irish language and the de-Anglicisation of Ireland.

Douglas Hyde's Gaelic League was not in existence when Anne Marie de Bovet visited Waterford, but she did notice the support of the Gaelic foot-ballers of Waterford and Kilkenny for the Irish National League, the organisa-tion set up by Parnell in 1882 as an alternative to the Land League. William O'Brien, the man who first proposed the Plan of Campaign, was one of the principal speakers at the I.N.L. meeting de Bovet attended. She wrote:

I WAS LUCKY enough to be present at one of those grand popular out-of-door meetings which constantly keep alive the spirit of rebellion in Ireland. These 'monster meetings', as they are called here, are announced weeks beforehand in all the villages of the adjacent counties, by placards headed with the three cabalistic letters, I.N.L.—Irish National League, with the war-cry of the Nationalists at the foot, 'God save Ireland!' At two o'clock the ceremony began with a carnival procession. First a squadron of farmers on horseback with green scarves; then trade unions, football clubs in striped jerseys of many colours, temperance societies, rural branches of the League, with flying banners embroidered with sacred subjects on a green ground, preceded by trumpets blowing with more spirit than accuracy, and a big drum overpowered by sharp fifes whose grating sound is not really so very disagreeable; then came a car on which was enthroned a very pretty girl, dressed entirely in green, leaning on a harp and personifying Erin; lastly, in several landaus, the Mayor and Corporation of Waterford accompanied the orators, of whom the principal were T. D. Sullivan, the poet member and William O'Brien, a hero of the Nationalist party. This procession, accompanied by the noise of crackers and deafening hurrahs, made the circuit of the town, which was decorated in Irish, French, and American flags—without an English one of course—and with trans-parencies of Mr Gladstone and Mr Parnell swinging from the top of be-ribanded and garlanded poles.

196

On the hill of Ballybricken was erected a rough wooden platform, decorated with evergreens and furnished with benches and chairs for the distinguished part of the audience—notables of the town with their wives, priests, journalists, a group of Liberal politicians of both sexes from England, come to see 'what sort of animals we look like at close quarters', as an Irish member said to me, laughing. In the centre a massive table served as a rostrum. Half-a-dozen ragged men armed with long sticks prevented ordinary mortals from invading the reserved enclosure; proud of their office, they acquitted themselves bravely, and turned out intruders with rough blows and vehement oaths. Over this vast space, crowded together round the platform, were twenty thousand eager listeners, mostly peasants, men, women and children.

By how many of those present could the orators hope to be heard? I have heard them put at one quarter, and I can easily believe it, at least as far as concerns Mr O'Brien, one of the most singular speakers I have ever heard. But all paid the most profound attention. A responsive crowd, if ever there was one, easily moved, inflammable, quick-witted and keen, understanding every hint, warm in its demonstrations, and interrupting frequently with the savage vociferation which here takes the place of applause, or with furious groans for some detested name, that, for example, of Mr Balfour, universally designated in the comic papers by the sobriquet of Clara. A mark of enthusiasm much in use here is a frantic twirling of handkerchiefs, generally dirty, held by one corner; when thousands of hands are simultaneously engaged in this manoeuvre the effect is most exhilarating. For three hours gushed the interminable Irish eloquence, William O'Brien first and foremost, with a vehemence of manner and a violence of expression contrasting curiously with the softness of his voice and the courtesy of his language off the platform. These passionate crowds require the eloquence of a tribune, and the Irish are past masters of the art. They smart for it sometimes. Absolute freedom of meeting is the corner-stone of British liberty, nevertheless the special repressive laws which the government is obliged to enact in Ireland, allow it to prosecute the authors of speeches outrageously seditious. This time no consequence of the kind troubled the orators, but Mr O'Brien was just released from a gaol in which he had been confined for four months, and was about to be imprisoned anew for a similar offence. Out of a hundred Irish Members of Parliament, there are generally half-a-dozen under lock and key. They find, it is true, some compensation in the intoxication of popularity and the sense of power. It is wonderful with what precision and dexterity they work the agitation, maintaining discipline among a people so excitable and so continually excited. In the course of this day, charged with the electricity of faction, I never saw the helmet of a constable; a reinforcement of two hundred and fifty men arrived the previous evening, but at the instance of the Mayor, who undertook to preserve order if the police did not interfere, the sheriff kept them carefully concealed. In the evening, at a public meeting in the town hall, two hundred persons assembled, and the speeches recommenced in the form of toasts, amid cheers and hurrahs without end, varied by national songs sung by some of the guests—a sort of ballad more sentimental than heroic, the words trivial and the music worthless. At midnight they were still haranguing, but I had given it up, and long afterwards the noise of their acclamations kept me awake in my room at the Imperial Hotel.

The excitement engendered by the new national movements ran high in the early nineties. Home Rule was the talking point in every home. The lot of the tenant farmers had been improved considerably by various land measures, and a new co-operative movement, based on the ideas of Horace Plunkett, a landlord recently returned from the American Mid-West, gave them further encouragement. While the Gaelic Athletic Association organised the country's manhood on the playing fields, the Gaelic League rekindled in the people an interest in their native language. Books and pamphlets in Irish were published, Irish classes were organised all over the country, and Oireachtas na Gaeilge, an annual Irish cultural festival, was founded. A lot of credit for the success of both the G.A.A. and the Gaelic League must be given to the humble country schoolmasters, such as the man the American traveller Clifton Johnson met while touring Ireland gathering material for his book *The Isle of the Shamrock* in the last decade of the century:

WE WENT in the waning evening light a mile or two up the valley. On ahead, looming hazily against the horizon sky, was one blue peak, but the view otherwise was of a bogland glen, barren and craggy, with a little river wandering through it, the scattered farm cabins clinging along the slopes. The master had a real affection for the valley, and was continually calling my attention to some phase of it—a glimpse of the stream, a curve of the road, or a green bush on a hillside—and asking if it was not beautiful. He seemed to be convinced that few landscapes could be more fair. We talked of America and we talked of Ireland, and we talked of the master's own trials and troubles. He complained resignedly of the monotony of his work, of the pay, which was only about sixty pounds a year, and of his having no associates but his few books. One of these books which had recently come into his possession was a cheap reprint of Bacon's *Essays*, and he was much impressed with the wisdom of the old philosopher and his quaint but forcible expression.

He had begun teaching when he was eighteen, and he had moved about here and there through the country, teaching ever since. The buildings he had taught in varied. Some were far better than this at Luckawn, and he mentioned one fine enough to cost two hundred pounds. On the other hand, in his earlier experiences, he had been much worse provided for, especially those times when he had taught a 'hedge' school—that is, had boarded around at the cottages, and made the kitchen of whatever house he happened to be living in serve for a schoolroom . . .

After my evening walk with the Luckawn schoolmaster, the only time I saw him was several days later, when I called one afternoon at the school-house. Lessons were over, and the master was marking in the scholars' books their tasks for the morrow. That finished, he told them to 'Begone!'

It was raining, and the boys put on their caps and buttoned their tattered coats closer, and the girls pulled their faded shawls over their heads. Then they all ran out into the storm with whoops of rejoicing. The master gave me the one chair. On his desk lay a paper printed in Irish. 'Ah,' he remarked, picking it up, 'that is as easy to me as English', and he read a half column aloud, in proof of his assertion. He sometimes wrote for the paper himself, both prose and poetry, he confided, taking a tin snuff-box from his pocket and indulging in a generous pinch; and he asked me what I thought of blank verse, double rhymes, etc.

At present he was composing a speech and a long poem, with the intention of journeying to Dublin a month or two later to recite them at the annual Irish literary festival. Perhaps I would like to hear them. He was evidently much pleased when I affirmed that I would, and said that to rehearse them

The schoolmaster described by Clifton Johnson

before a stranger would help give him courage for the great occasion to come. He cleared his throat and adjusted a red handkerchief in the outer breast pocket of his overcoat so that the corner showed; he felt of his necktie, and he pulled his spectacles down on his nose from where they had been reposing amid the ruffled hair on the top of his head. Then a doubt occurred to him. 'What do you think,' he inquired, 'would it be better to wear or not to wear specs?'

I expressed the opinion that it would be all right either way, and he said personally he preferred to wear them. He was not used to speaking in public, and through his 'specs' he saw the audience more dimly and was less timid; but he believed the impression on his hearers was better with them off. The latter thought was conclusive, and he laid them on his desk. Then he drew himself together and began. His voice changed with the changing sentiments of the words, but his prevailing tones were gentle and melancholy. In the attitude assumed at the start he stood looking straight ahead, with hands interlocked and at rest before him. Gestures, however, soon began to come thick and fast, that which recurred most frequently consisting in clasping one or both hands to his heart.

The speech was on the revival of the Irish language, the poem a general glorification of Erin. At least, so the master described them. I had no other clue, for they were in the ancient Gaelic. At the close of each peroration he inquired with concern, was it slow enough, was I pleased with the sound of it, could I tell just how long it had taken by my watch.

When I left the schoolhouse a little later I bade the schoolmaster a final good-by, and the next morning I resumed my journey—but I shall never forget him. He was a simple and earnest soul, mistaken perhaps in his conception of the necessity of sternness and violence in teaching, yet at heart sound. It is not, however, so much the teacher that I recall, as the literary enthusiast and scholar rehearsing his Irish speech and poem in the dusk of his old battered schoolroom. He made a pathetic figure—tall and hollow-chested, his shabby clothes hanging limply about him, and in his eyes a vague far-away look, showing that in spirit he was declaiming before the Dublin audience. After all, the golden glow of hope and aspiration can shine amid the boglands just as brightly as anywhere else in the world.

Dublin was, of course, the nerve centre of the great revival. It had little effect on the north-east, where, then as now, civil discord and religious strife was the main news of the day. Ever since the Orange and Green factions agreed to co-operate in repealing the Party Processions Bill, thereby allowing both factions to stage their parades, rioting occurred frequently. Dr Macaulay, in his 1872 *Tour of Observation*, had this to say about the parades of that year:

BEFORE THE processions of 1872 began in Ireland, an earnest appeal was made to the Orangemen to desist from party irritation. The Catholics solemnly declared that they would not interfere with any Orange demonstration, but as firmly stated that for every Protestant procession they would have a larger Catholic procession. What is to be the end of a rivalry like this? Law cannot check it, and the only hope is in an improved state of public opinion. There are not wanting signs of this improvement being seen. The ruffians who interfered with the Catholic procession of 15 August in Belfast belonged to no recognised organisation. It was stated by the prison chaplain, that among the numerous prisoners there was not one Presbyterian. The ship-carpenters who were charged as a body with having taken a large part in the riots, through the committee of their trade society, repudiated the accusation. The interference, which resulted in so much mischief, seems to have been commenced by a rabble who, if Orangemen, were a disgrace to the name and the cause . . .

The disturbers of the procession ought to have been dealt with summarily, and a little severity at the moment would have proved mercy in the end. *The Times*, commenting on the riots, made the same reference to American precedent: 'A Catholic procession in the north of Ireland, acting within the limits of the law, may claim a similar escort, and the Executive Government would be justified in sending it, whether claimed or not. If under such circumstances Orangemen attempted to stop the procession, and declined to disperse when duly warned, they should be fired upon. Less than this we cannot do without conniving at organised lawlessness calling itself Protestant Christianity; whether we ought to do more is a matter on which we are not at present compelled to pronounce an opinion.'

Whatever may be intended by this writer as to ulterior measures, it is plain that the disturbance is kept up by a comparatively small section of the people. The numbers seen at a procession are gathered from a wide extent of country, the two parties striving in emulation to make an imposing display of numbers as well as of banners and insignia.

All respectable citizens, except fanatics in religion or politics, condemn these party demonstrations; commerce and business suffer, and the payments of rates and expenses will impose no light penalty on districts and towns which have been the scenes of violence.

Despite the discord, however, Belfast continued to prosper. Some of the travellers who visited it in the last quarter of the century thought it a more cheerful place than Dublin, and it was generally agreed that the poor of Belfast were better fed and better housed than their counterparts in the southern city. Anne Marie de Bovet found Dublin particularly depressing, a city where the middle classes were growing prosperous and where the poor remained as poor as they had been when the Halls visited the city before the famine. Wrote de Bovet:

DEAR, DIRTY DUBLIN! Such are the familiar terms—now become proverbial—in which Lady Morgan, in her writings, apostrophizes her native town. Dear dirty Dublin is nothing more than a conglomeration of poor quarters, whose misery overflows on to the doorsteps of the rich, resembling in that respect the cities of former times, where the classes elbowed each other much more than they do in the towns of this democratic age. I was speaking a short while ago of the beggars that haunt O'Connell Street. They are to be seen everywhere, on the bridges, on the quays, round the squares, leaning over the parapets, and standing against the railings watching the running water and the passers-by, a greasy felt hat over one ear, their hands in the pockets of their trousers, which are

Saturday night in Dublin, 1890

fringed out below, with holes at the knees. The upper portion is happily hidden by a dirty jacket full of holes, through which the lining is often protruding. There are greater numbers of boys here than anywhere else in prolific Ireland. They go about in troops, dressed in a waistcoat innocent of buttons, and in seatless breeches—a deficiency all the more to be regretted, because the shirt, when there is one, owing to successive simplications has been reduced to a bodice only; socks, shoes and caps are unknown luxuries— human skin is less expensive than shoemakers' leather, and the mass of tangles, which occasionally sees the comb on a Sunday, is given by nature as a covering for the head against rain as well as sun.

The girls are more dignified in their princess dresses of velvet, which once were ruby or blue, old cast-offs of more fortunate children who are grand-mothers now. These sumptuous garments are invariably covered up with an apron, which has never been white, and it is so full of holes that it is very easy to account for the numerous dirty spots on the dress. These young people frequent, by preference, the fine streets, and glue their noses to the shop fronts, specially those which sell sugar-candy, burnt almonds, and those abominations in coloured starch which Dublin confectioners insult us by calling 'Bonbons Francais'. Morning and evening they sell newspapers; between whiles, they look out for windfalls. In Dublin, begging is forbidden, and is only carried on under some disguise. So, tall fine-looking girls, with clogs and a straw hat and feathers, offer to the passers-by little bunches of pale geraniums, withered Indian pinks, anaemic-looking asters, and blighted dahlias; of course, one pays no attention to them, so that without losing any-thing their stock-in-trade lasts a good week. They will take no refusal, and beg you to give them a cup of tea.

The idea of sitting down in their company in the tea-house close by appears to you preposterous, so you give them a copper; and if you happen to turn your head, you will have the satisfaction of seeing them solacing themselves with a mug of porter at the public-house opposite. The dress of the poorest women in Dublin defies all description—not one has ever worn garments that have been made for her; in fact there does not exist here, not even in the most populous parts of the town, cheap haberdashery shops, where, as with us, poor women can buy a skirt, and a worsted or cotton bodice. They dress here on the 'reach-me-down' system; the demand for rags is so enormous that if the cast-off clothes of every country in the world were imported into Ireland they would hardly suffice. These rags are the more hideous too, by reason of the materials of which they are made—silk skirts all befrilled, shining with grease, and with more holes than a sieve; velvet cloaks of an indefinable colour, with jet embroidery on one side and silk fringe on the other, worn and rusty, stiff with grease, and moth-eaten; plush hats, once grey-green, trimmed with something that in the prehistoric ages might have been a bunch of feathers, or, perhaps, a wreath of roses. Believe me, I do not exaggerate. As for women of a better class—workwomen, small shopkeepers, well-to-do householders—if they are a little less dirty they are hardly less ragged. Irishwomen have a passion for furbelows, which is only equalled by their ignorance of the use of needle and thread. Here is the result: a frill that has become unsewn they will draggle in the mud for hours; when some spare moment arrives, and they have had the good luck to find a pin on the ground, they will fasten it up with that; and so things will remain until, eventually, the frill is overweighted with dirt, and comes off altogether. For the rest, though they are indifferent to going about barelegged, it would be a disgrace to them to go out bareheaded, and as the cap and little bonnet of our women are unknown here, a greasy hood bound with crumpled strings tied under the chin, or a large straw hat on which nods a limp and discoloured feather, is to them the mark of *respectability*. But to see the abject squalor of Dublin in its very depths one had only to walk along by St Patrick's, and particularly the street which joins the two cathedrals—a street consisting of two rows of tumble-down, mouldy-looking houses, reeking of dirt, and oozing with the disgusting smell of accumulated filth of many generations, with old petticoats hung up instead of curtains, and very often instead of glass in the dilapidated windows. On each ground floor, shops with overhanging roofs, and resembling dirty cellars, expose for sale sides of rancid bacon, bundles of candles and jars of treacle—a delicacy as much sought after as soap is neglected—greens, cauliflowers, musty turnips and bad potatoes; while at every three doors is a tavern, which in the midst of these hovels resembles a palace. Every other house is an old-clothes shop where the sale of the above-mentioned rags is combined with money-lending at large interest. Shoes that are taken out of pawn there on Saturday night for Sunday Mass are pledged again on Monday morning. Business is as brisk there all Sunday as it is during the week.

Most of the rag-dealers being Jews, as is the custom of the children of

The Liberties, Dublin, 1890

Israel, they understand their business, and are the only fat and flourishing inhabitants of St Patrick Street. Their crowded shops are the clubs of the place. The purchase of a pair of trousers, a petticoat or a shirt—which, to judge by the length of time it takes, seems a most complicated business—is only an excuse for gossiping, with that wild intemperance, that super-abundance of exclamation and expletives that the Irish have in common with southern races. On the pavements, strewn with vegetable refuse and other mess, a permanent market is held. There are barrels of red herrings, pickled in brine: flat baskets, in which are spread out the most disgusting bits of meat that one can possibly imagine; stale cows' feet; overkept sheeps' heads, bits of flabby pink veal, tripe, intestines, skins, and fat of every animal eatable and otherwise—refuse that no well-trained dog would touch. Besides being made quite sick with the smell of this filthy food, mixed with that of bad cabbage, tobacco and petroleum, which comes out in puffs from the half-opened hovels, the passer-by is tormented by an uneasy feeling of being devoured. But the tourist forgets all this while lingering in this Court of Miracles, from whose many aspects an artist, who was courageous enough to stay there some time, might find very amusing subjects for water-colour sketches. His endurance must be all the greater, because the curiosity with which he will inspire this lazy population will quickly gather round him a crowd, whose close contact will put his olfactory nerves to a severe trial. But all these ragged and vermin-covered people are most affable; there are none of those fierce looks, those looks of hatred with which in other countries the poor welcome 'the rich' who happen to have missed their way among them; on the contrary they are very pleased when ladies and gentlemen think it worth while to visit them. They look at them with a curiosity which is neither low-bred nor insolent, require very little encouragement to be made to talk, and willingly shake hands with the good-natured stranger who will sacrifice his gloves. Far from being ashamed of their rags, they are proud of being looked at; pretty, fair, or red-haired girls, whose freshness has not yet been spoilt by bad air, insufficient food, or drinking to excess, nudge each other, laughing and blushing; cheeky children come and stare at you, under your very nose, and vanish like a flock of sparrows if you pretend to be angry; mothers smile at you gratefully if you glance tenderly at the baby. It is a question, which we do not yet feel competent to answer, as to how far these poor people are responsible for the abject state of misery in which they are plunged; but it touches one to see the good temper, sociableness, and even politeness that survive such degradation.

St Patrick Street may be called the *Boulevard des Italiens* of the quarter known as 'the Liberties' of Dublin, where grovel the five or six thousand inhabitants I have just been describing. Situated in the highest, airiest, and consequently the healthiest part of the town, it was once the aristocratic centre. For some extraordinary reason it has been deserted for the low and damp parts of the estuary of the Liffey called *The Black Pool,* a black marsh. The gardens have disappeared, the fine houses have fallen into ruins, those which still remain are transformed into human rookeries, and under the finger of time are crumbling away. The streets are connected by a network of stinking little alleys and infected courts, where wretched hens and lean goats pick about among the refuse. What one sees in the interiors makes one sick and sad at the same time. One day the sanitary officers found in a large bare room eighteen human beings, huddled together asleep on the floor, whose only furniture was their bundles and a few bits of dirty straw. In the next room were lodged twelve, seven of whom were ill with typhoid fever.

The population of Belfast rose from one hundred thousand in 1851 to approximately three hundred and ten thousand in the year of de Bovet's visit. Dublin's population had increased an approximate twenty-five per cent in the same period, to about three hundred and eighty thousand. The population of most other Irish towns had, however, declined, and a large part of the labour force in both capital and provincial towns were casual, under-paid workers.

De Bovet did not notice any significant new ideas stirring the conscience of the Dublin of 1890. Had she arrived at the end of the decade she might have commented on the impact of the city's two new papers. In one of these, *The United Irishman*, a middle-class printer named Griffith, whose sympathies lay with capital, preached a doctrine of self-reliance which would, it was argued, turn Ireland into a thriving industrial state, politically and economically independent; in the other, *The Workers' Republic*, the founder of the Irish Socialist Republican Party, James Connolly, advocated rebellion to break the hold of British capitalist imperialism. She might, too, have told us about the new school of Anglo-Irish poets and playwrights who found inspiration in the efforts of the Gaelic League: a school whose greatest glory was William Butler Yeats.

But as the nineteenth century died, no observer could possibly have foreseen the possibilities of a fusion of all the elements that reflected a new awareness of Irish nationality: who would dream that the editor of *The Workers' Republic* and the disciples of the printer of *The United Irishman* would join, sixteen years into the new century, with the Gaelic Leaguer, Pearse, the old Fenian Tom Clarke, and the G.A.A. man Collins, in revolution: and that the ascendancy poet Yeats would be among the first to praise the gallantry of their attempt at Easter to shake the blossom from the bud?

List of sources

Rev. Thomas Armstrong, *My Life in Connacht*, 1906
A. Atkinson, *The Irish Tourist*, 1815
John Barrow, *A Tour Round Ireland*, 1836
William Barry, *A Walking Tour of Ireland*
Gustave de Beaumont, *L'Irlande Sociale Politique et Religieuse*, 1839
Bernard H. Becker, *Disturbed Ireland*, 1881
William Bennett, *Narrative of a Recent Journey of Six Weeks in Ireland*, 1847
Henry Arthur Blake (Terence McGrath), *Pictures from Ireland*, 1880
Anne Marie de Bovet, *Three Months' Tour in Ireland*, 1891
Sir John Carr, *The Stranger in Ireland*, 1806
Lady Chatterton, *Rambles in the South of Ireland*, 1839
Thomas Crofton Croker, *Researches in the South of Ireland*, 1824
John Gough, *A Tour in Ireland in 1813 and 1814*, 1817
Mr & Mrs S. C. Hall, *Ireland Its Scenery and Character*, 1841–3 (3 vols.)
Spencer T. Hall, *Life and Death in Ireland as Witnessed in 1849*, 1850
Philip Hardy, *Lettres sur les Elections Anglaises et sur la Situation de l'Irlande*, 1827
Mrs M. C. Houstoun, *Twenty Years in the Wild West*, 1879
Henry Inglis, *A Journey throughout Ireland during the Spring, Summer and Autumn of 1834*, 1834
Clifton Johnson, *The Isle of the Shamrock*, 1901
Dr James Johnson, *A Tour in Ireland with Meditations and Reflections*, 1844
J. L. Joynes, *The Adventures of a Tourist in Ireland*, 1882
Johann Georg Köhl, *Reisen in Ireland*, 1843
J. G. Lockhart, *Memoirs of the Life of Sir Walter Scott*, 1847
Baron E. de Mandat-Grancey, *Paddy at Home*, 1887
James Macaulay, *Ireland in 1872—A Tour of Observation*, 1873
Randall M'Collum, *Sketches of the Highlands of Cavan taken during the Irish Famine*, 1856
Harriet Martineau, *Letters from Ireland*, 1852
Mrs. Asenath Nicholson, *Ireland's Welcome to the Stranger*, 1847
Prince Hermann Ludwig Heinrich Von Pückler-Muskau, *Tour in England, Ireland and France in 1828 and 1829*, translated by Sarah Austin, 1832
Anne Plumptre, *Narrative of a Residence in Ireland during the Summer of 1814 and that of 1815*
Dr Samuel Reynolds Hole, *A Little Tour in Ireland*, 1859
William Makepeace Thackeray, *The Irish Sketch Book*, 1843
Charlotte Elizabeth Tonna, *Letters from Ireland*, 1838
Edwin Trueman, *Notes on a Trip to Ireland*, 1890